WITHDRAWN

St. Louis Community College

Library

5801 Wilson Avenue
St. Louis, Missouri 63110

DIGITAL AUDIO
ENGINEERING
An Anthology

THE COMPUTER MUSIC and DIGITAL AUDIO SERIES

John Strawn, Series Editor

DIGITAL AUDIO SIGNAL PROCESSING: An Anthology
Edited by John Strawn
with contributions by J. W. Gordon, F. R. Moore, J. A. Moorer,
T. L. Petersen, J. O. Smith, and J. Strawn

COMPOSERS AND THE COMPUTER
Edited by Curtis Roads
with contributions by or about H. Brün, J. Chowning, J. Dashow,
C. Dodge, P. Hamlin, G. Lewis, T. Machover, J.-C. Risset, C. Roads,
and I. Xenakis

DIGITAL AUDIO ENGINEERING: An Anthology
Edited by John Strawn
with contributions by J. McGill, F. R. Moore, J. A. Moorer, P. Samson,
and R. Talambiras

THE LITTLE BOOK OF COMPUTER MUSIC INSTRUMENTS
Dexter Morrill

A COMPUTER MUSIC HISTORY
Curtis Roads

COMPUTER APPLICATIONS IN MUSIC: A Bibliography
Deta S. Davis

DIGITAL AUDIO ENGINEERING
An Anthology

JOHN STRAWN, Editor

with contributions by

JAMES F. MCGILL
ROBERT TALAMBIRAS
PETER R. SAMSON
F. RICHARD MOORE
JAMES A. MOORER

WILLIAM KAUFMANN, INC.
Los Altos, California

Library of Congress Cataloging in Publication Data
Main entry under title:

Digital audio engineering.

  (The Computer music and digital audio series)
  Bibliography: p.
  Includes index.
  1. Sound—Recording and reproducing—Digital techniques.
2. Synthesizer (Musical instrument) I. Strawn, John,
1950–   . II. McGill, James F. III. Series.
TK7881.4.D53   1985   621.389'3   85-18
ISBN 0-86576-087-X

William Kaufmann, Inc.
95 First Street
Los Altos, California 94022

10   9   8   7   6   5   4   3   2   1

CONTENTS

CONTRIBUTORS

JAMES F. MCGILL, Digital Sound, 2030 Alameda Padre Serra, Santa Barbara, Calif. 93103.

F. RICHARD MOORE, Department of Music B-026, University of California at San Diego, La Jolla, Calif. 92093.

JAMES A. MOORER, The Droid Works, Post Office Box CS 8180, San Rafael, Calif. 94912.

PETER R. SAMSON, Systems Concepts, 520 Third Street, San Francisco, Calif. 94107.

ROBERT TALAMBIRAS, 58 Sherwood Road, Springfield, N.J. 07081.

A NOTE
ABOUT THIS SERIES

The Computer Music and Digital Audio Series has been established to serve as a central source for books dealing with computer music, digital audio, and related subjects.

During the past few decades, computer music and digital audio have developed as closely related fields that draw from a wide variety of disciplines: audio engineering, computer science, digital signal processing and hardware, psychology (especially perception), physics, and of course all aspects of music.

The series includes, but is not limited to

- textbooks (at the undergraduate and graduate levels)
- guides for audio engineers and studio musicians
- how-to books (such as collections of patches for synthesis)
- anthologies (such as the present volume)
- reference works and monographs
- books for home computer users and synthesizer players

The present volume is one of three anthologies published in 1985 to inaugurate the series. Together, they cover subject matter that has not yet been covered in such breadth and depth. A number of other manuscripts are already in preparation; we anticipate that two or three volumes will appear each year for the next several years.

I should like to express my deepest appreciation to John Snell and Curtis Roads, who played a significant role in collecting some of the material for these first three volumes, and who provided valuable editorial assistance; to my colleagues in computer music and digital audio, especially at CCRMA, for their help and advice; and to William Kaufmann and his fine staff, who have the vision, patience, and professional commitment needed for changing a series editor's rough ideas into finely crafted works in print.

John Strawn
Stanford, California

PREFACE

The advent of digital audio represents one of the most significant advances in recording technology since Edison's generation. All of the traditional recording processes produce a copy of the original air pressure wave that makes sound. Digital audio recording takes a series of samples, akin to snapshots, of that pressure wave at a very high rate. Each sample is stored digitally (as a number) on tape, on a disk, or in computer memory. When desired, the original signal can be reconstructed from the numbers stored digitally.

Compared with traditional analog technology, digital audio results in a considerable improvement in quality for the consumer. Digital audio can be mixed and processed without significant addition of noise. Moreover, a digital recording can be copied repeatedly without adding to the noise level (in other words, digital audio dispenses with cumulative tape hiss). Given the proper investment in hardware, audio distortion can be reduced to negligible levels.

Digital music synthesis and processing confront the same implementation problems as digital audio recording and reproduction. When a recording engineer is mixing several tracks, or when a composer is processing previously recorded material as part of a composition, enormous demands are made on the digital hardware and software. In lay terms, the hardware must be able to handle perhaps 50 000 numbers per second per channel. This happens because the human auditory system can perceive frequencies up to about 20 000 Hz. Because of the effects treated by the sampling theorem, the sample rate must be at least twice as fast as the highest frequency to be handled. Some overhead must be allowed as well. The hardware must take care of all of the mixing and processing for every incoming channel of sound at this high data rate.

This book concentrates on such engineering aspects of high-quality digital audio processing and synthesis. (Applications based on microcomputers were given a thorough treatment by Chamberlin [1980]). Much of the work discussed here has been motivated by computer music synthesis, a field in which a considerable amount of experience working with digital audio has already been gathered. Further information on these rapidly developing areas can be found in the pages of the *Journal of the Audio Engineering Society, Studio Sound, Mix, Recording Engineering/Producer, Digital Audio, Keyboard,* and *Computer Music Journal.*

James McGill (chapter 1 in this volume) provides a solid technical introduction to the process of digital audio recording and reproduction, covering such basic issues as sampling and A-law, μ-law, and floating-point quantization. McGill provides an especially thorough treatment of the design of (analog) input and output filters. The chapter continues with a discussion of sample rates and closes by exploring issues in coding schemes.

Robert Talambiras' chapter (chapter 2) complements that of McGill. Talambiras discusses dynamic range as a function of the accuracy (number of bits) of the digital audio system. Moving quickly to practical systems, he discusses no less than twenty-five sources of noise in the digital recording/reproduction process, and weighs the relative merits of various solutions to these noise problems. The extensive references in both of these chapters provide the interested reader with opportunity for further exploration.

Consumer audio is already converting to digital playback systems, so it is understandable that the recording studio is likewise being converted to digital. A central component of a digital recording studio is a digital audio processor. Such a unit can also function as a synthesizer for producing music and sound effects. Three such synthesizer/processor designs are discussed in this volume.

In the early days of computer music, a number of small- and medium-sized digital synthesizers were developed. These included commercial devices such as the Synclavier and the Fairlight keyboard synthesizers as well as units in institutions such as the University of Toronto and the University of Aarhus, Denmark. These designs have been documented elsewhere, such as in the references cited earlier or in Roads and Strawn (1985). The first truly massive digital synthesizer was designed and constructed by Peter Samson and installed at the Center for Computer Research in Music and Acoustics (CCRMA), Stanford University. It has been in use since 1977 for instruction, research, composition, and live performance; works synthesized on this device can be heard on the various tapes, records, and compact disks produced by CCRMA.

The Samson Box, as it is known, is a time-multiplexed, pipelined machine with 256 digital oscillators plus digital hardware for filtering, reverberation, and the like. In his chapter in this volume, Samson opens with a discussion of the overall constraints on the hardware design, especially budgetary limitations and performance requirements. He offers insights into many design decisions, such as which synthesis techniques to implement directly or whether to use fixed- or floating-point arithmetic. The chapter includes a discussion of the accuracy of representing various quantities, such as frequency and amplitude. Samson also explores the implementation of filters, schemes for connecting various functional units, and issues related to I/O with the host computer. In particular, synthesizers of this type are controlled by a stream of commands. Samson's chapter discusses the general question of the command rate necessary to sustain complex music, as well as details of the command format for this particular device.

In the fourth chapter, F. Richard Moore presents another audio processor architecture, one which emphasizes the capability of changing hardware fairly easily as new demands arise, such as with the developement of new synthesis techniques. In a word, this is a modular system; Moore gives details on specific modules as well as on the means for connecting and controlling them. This device is now in the Center for Music Experiment at the University of California at San Diego. Moore's chapter includes a review of the GROOVE machine at Bell Laboratories, which he helped develop and which was the forerunner of all interactive digital audio systems.

James Moorer discusses engineering solutions to film sound processing in the final chapter in this volume. Film sound includes background music, speech (recorded on location or in a studio), and sound effects, recorded or synthesized. Mixing sound for film is complicated by the fact that the visual image may be changed very late in the process; remixing the individual sound tracks at such a late stage has often been impossible with previous technology.

Use of digital technology simplifies this process significantly. At Lucasfilm, Moorer has designed and constructed the Audio Signal Processor (ASP). In his chapter, Moorer gives an overview of the entire Lucasfilm digital studio setup, and provides details on the ASP. This architecture is based on functional units hung between buses, under microcode control. Moorer also gives details of the individual units, and treats I/O and storage questions in the context of film sound production. The ASP has already been in use, and will be available commercially.

REFERENCES

Chamberlin, Hal. 1980. *Musical applications of microprocessors.* Rochelle Park, N.J.: Hayden.

Roads, Curtis, and John Strawn, eds. 1985. *Foundations of computer music.* Cambridge: MIT Press.

1

AN INTRODUCTION
TO DIGITAL
RECORDING AND
REPRODUCTION

James F. McGill

HISTORICAL OVERVIEW

Sound is one of the primary means of communication between human beings. Speech and music have written notation,
but in both cases the symbols provide only a partial representation of the information conveyed by sound. With recording
machines, however, it becomes possible to store and recall a
more or less exact reproduction of sound, complete with all
the nuance that is lost in written transcription.

The means for recording sound dates back to Thomas Alva
Edison who patented the phonograph in 1877. The subsequent one hundred years of technical developments can be

1

split conceptually into two fifty-year phases: the period from 1877 to 1927 and the period from 1927 to 1977. During the first phase, mechanoacoustical principles formed the basis for sound recording technology. The storage medium was etched foil or engraved wax, and record and playback amplification was by means of acoustical horns.

The confluence of several fundamental inventions during this first fifty-year phase established the foundation for a transition to electrical, rather than mechanical, recording machines. Valdemar Poulsen, a Danish engineer, developed the first magnetic tape recorder in 1898. This machine had no amplifiers and no biasing; nevertheless, it marked the beginning of the electromagnetic recording technique. Still, wide acceptance of the technology and high-quality recording had to wait for several other engineering contributions. Sir John Ambrose Fleming took another discovery of Edison's and made it useful when he developed the diode vacuum tube in 1904. Lee DeForest, in 1907, developed the vacuum tube amplifier. The microphone and loudspeaker were developed in the twenties, along with the technique of bias recording. It turned out that yet another Edison invention, the motion picture, provided the final impetus for the transition to electrical recording machines. In 1927, *Birth of A Nation,* the first motion picture with sound, appeared and this marked the beginning of the second fifty-year phase of sound recording history.

These innovations of the first fifty years established the direction for the second fifty years of sound recording. During this second period the original mechanoacoustical recorders and playback units were completely superseded by electroacoustical devices. However, even with the introduction of electrical recording, the basic scheme for encoding the sound remained the same as it had been in the original mechanical recorders. This scheme is called *analog recording* because it is based on storing a signal analogous to the sound waveform.

In the seventies digital recording machines became available. These machines are based on an encoding scheme which, for the first time in one hundred years, is a departure from the original analog method of Edison. Digital recorders preserve sound as a series of numbers, each of which accurately describes the acoustical waveform at a particular instant in time. At first glance this may seem like a cumbersome approach, but in fact it proves to be superior to conventional recording techniques in every way.

It is interesting to note that the theoretical foundation for digital recording of sound has been evolving since before Edison's original sound recorder of 1877, but the technology required to implement the theoretical results has only recently become feasible. The sampling theorem, which is attributed to Nyquist, was apparently first stated by Cauchy (1841). Hartley's law, which gives the information capacity of an ideal channel, appeared in 1928, as did Nyquist's results. Reeves (1938) implemented the first pulse-code-modulation system, making use of the theoretical concepts of his predecessors. Shannon (1948) presented two powerful theorems, one on information coding and one extending Hartley's results to a noise-contaminated channel. Hamming (1950) and Gilbert (1960) presented seminal work on error correction schemes. Huffman (1952) described a minimum redundancy coding scheme. In the sixties and seventies Sato, Blesser, Stockham, Doi, and others made contributions which resulted finally in the reduction to practice of digital recording of sound (see also Nakajima et al. 1983).

FUNDAMENTALS

The function of a recording system is the storage of information. The information may derive from video or film images, music, speech, or any other source of data. For the purposes of this chapter, only sound recording will be considered; however, many of the concepts discussed here apply equally well to any form of information.

Recording systems can be divided into two generic classes: *analog* and *digital*. The distinction between these two classes lies in the means of representation of the recorded information. An analog system stores a continuous representation, whereas a digital system stores a discretely sampled and quantized representation. The subject of this chapter is digital recording, so from here on only the digital systems will be described.

Typical Recording Systems

The capabilities required in a digital recording system are *data conversion* and *data storage.* Such systems also may include *data transmission* and *data processing* capabilities. Many types of digital recording systems have been optimized for different requirements, but they can all be analyzed in terms of the capabilities just mentioned.

Figure 1.1 shows the block diagram of a typical digital recording system. The incoming signal is converted to digital form by an analog-to-digital converter. The digital signal is then encoded and formatted into blocks for storage. The reproduced signal is recalled from storage, deformatted, decoded, and converted via a digital-to-analog converter. Each functional block in figure 1.1 represents a great deal of hidden detail which is discussed in following sections.

Sampling and Quantization

The Fundamental Theorem of Sampling (Nyquist 1928; Linden 1959) states that a band-limited continuous waveform can be exactly represented by a set of

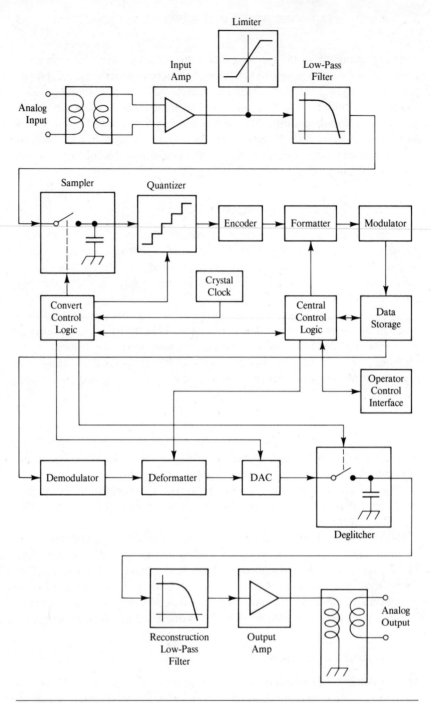

Fig. 1.1. Functional block diagram of a typical digital recording system

discrete samples of the waveform, provided the sampling frequency is at least twice the highest frequency present in the original waveform. Stated quantitatively, a signal of bandwidth f_N and duration T can be represented exactly by $2f_N T$ equally spaced samples. While this result seems rather amazing, Oliver (in Oliver et al. 1948) has pointed out that the same signal can also be represented by exactly $2f_N T$ Fourier coefficients.

Sampling is a time-domain process that yields a sequence of pulses representing a signal at discrete instants of time. *Quantization* is the representation of signal amplitude by certain discrete allowed levels. The data conversion process involves time sampling and quantization of the time samples, yielding a sequence of quantized samples. For purposes of analysis the distinction between sampling and quantization must be kept clear. It is a common practice in the literature (e.g., Bennett 1948) to use the term *quantization* to indicate the combined result of sampling and amplitude quantization. This convention is not followed in this chapter; the combined process is referred to as *analog-to-digital conversion* or *digitization*. Figure 1.2 illustrates the quantization of a simple waveform and shows the transfer function of the quantizer.

The fidelity of a digital recording system is dependent upon the system sampling frequency and the accuracy of the system quantizer. This dependency is discussed in detail later; but in general terms, the sample frequency determines the system bandwidth and the accuracy of the quantizer determines the system distortion and dynamic range.

DATA CONVERSION

In general, the object of a data conversion system is twofold. On the input (or analog-to-digital) side, a continuous signal is filtered, sampled, quantized, and encoded into a digital representation. On the output (or digital-to-analog) side, a digital signal is converted to a sequence of impulses which are low-pass filtered to yield a reconstruction of the original signal.

All practical data conversion systems must operate at a rate high enough to satisfy the sampling theorem requirement, but beyond that commonality there are many different variations. This section describes some standard data conversion techniques. For a further description of these techniques, as well as others not discussed in this chapter (e.g., delta modulation and its variants), see the collection of papers edited by Jayant (1976) and Blesser's excellent review (1978) on the subject of data conversion.

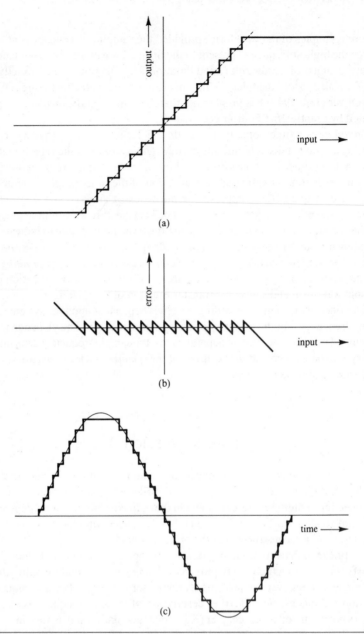

Fig. 1.2. Quantization. (a) Transfer function for a uniform quantizer. (b) Quantization error for a ramp input. (c) Quantized sine wave.

Pulse-Code Modulation

Pulse-code modulation (PCM) was invented by Reeves (1938). The most important early papers on the subject were by Bennett (1948) and by Oliver et al. (1948).

The coding of a signal by PCM involves the following steps:

1. Filtering: In order to satisfy the sampling theorem the incoming signal must be band-limited. This is accomplished by low-pass filtering the signal.
2. Sampling: The band-limited signal is sampled at a frequency at least twice the highest signal frequency. This sampling must occur with a very narrow time aperture in order that the signal does not change significantly during the sampling process. The sample interval (time between successive samples) must be very constant to avoid time-base errors (which will manifest themselves as noise components in the converted signal).
3. Quantization: The amplitude of each signal sample is quantized into one of the allowed quantizer levels. Notice that a deliberate error is imparted to the signal at this point by approximating the actual signal amplitude by a quantized value. If all components in the PCM system are ideal and distortionless, the system distortion is set by this quantization error.
4. Encoding: The quantized signal samples are represented by digital code words. For a binary code, if the quantizer has 2^M discrete levels, then the code word needs to be M bits in length. Each of the 2^M possible code words represents one of the states of the quantizer.
5. Decoding: In order to reconstruct the original signal the encoded samples are converted into a sequence of impulses. This operation is performed by a digital-to-analog converter as shown in figure 1.3. The impulses are separated in time by the same sample period that was used in the encoding. Each impulse has an amplitude equal to the quantized sample amplitude as stored in the encoded sample sequence. The sequence of impulses is low-pass filtered with a cutoff frequency less than half of the sample frequency. A proof that this reconstructed signal is identical to the original signal is also a proof of the sampling theorem. This can be found several places in the literature (cf. Oliver et al. 1948) and therefore is not repeated here.

Figure 1.1 includes the block diagram of a PCM encoder and decoder. The input signal is buffered and filtered. A sample-hold amplifier performs the sampling function and the analog-to-digital (ADC) components do the quantization and the encoding. For decoding, the digital-to-analog converter (DAC) component converts the digital signal to a sequence of proportional impulses.

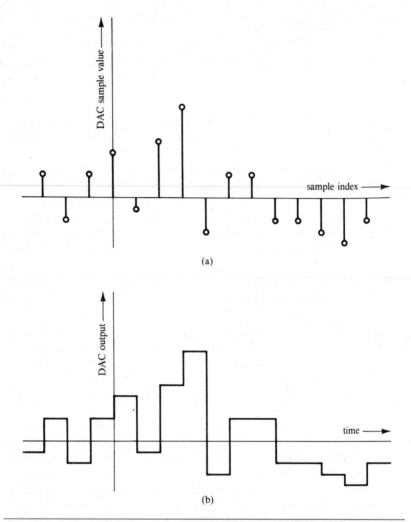

Fig. 1.3. Transfer function for an ideal zero-order hold digital-to-analog converter (DAC). (a) Digital-to-analog output. (b) Zero-order hold output.

The deglitcher is an element that keeps DAC switching transients from degrading the output signal. A reconstruction low-pass filter rejects all but baseband signal components, and the filter output is buffered to provide the decoder output signal.

In most PCM systems the quantizer has equally spaced levels, giving a uniform distribution of states across the amplitude range of the system. For an

M-bit system there are 2^M such quantization states. It can be shown (Blesser 1978, Talambiras 1985) that the full-scale signal-to-noise ratio (SNR) of such a system is given by

$$SNR(dB) \cong 6.02M + 1.76, \tag{1.1}$$

where the quantization error amplitude distribution is assumed to be uniform over all allowed error values. This result indicates that each bit in the system contributes about 6 dB of SNR, a result which is reasonable since each bit doubles the total number of quantization states and 6 dB corresp   ctor of 2.

Overload is an important issue in PCM systems. Any ir   at exceeds the range of the quantizer must be clipped at the ex   er levels; obviously this produces gross distortion. To avoid su   n-nett (1948) suggested 2 bits, or 12 dB, of headroom between i   it levels and full scale. His argument was based on experimen   f thermal noise which he said never appreciably exceeded four times r   t such a nominal level the SNR given above decreases by 9 dB to the re   n by Jayant (1964),

$$SNR_{4\sigma}(dB) \cong 6.02M - 7.2.$$

This condition is referred to as *four-sigma loading* because for signals with gaussian statistics the rms is equal to the standard deviation which is designated by the Greek letter sigma.

In typical recording studies the average signal level is 8 to 24 dB below full scale, with the actual number dependent upon the program material being recorded and the inclinations of the recording engineer. The figure of 24 dB corresponds to 4 bits in a PCM system, or *sixteen-sigma* loading, and the SNR at nominal input level for such a system is

$$SNR_{16\sigma}(dB) \cong 6.02M - 19.2.$$

For example, a 16-bit system has a theoretical SNR of 77.1 dB with sixteen-sigma loading.

The dynamic range of a PCM system is given by equation 1.1; it equals the SNR for a full-scale input signal. For example, a 16-bit system has a theoretical dynamic range of 98.08 dB.

Nonuniform Quantization

Several types of data conversion systems have quantizers with levels which are nonuniformly distributed over the range of input signal levels. In general these systems establish a higher density of quantization states for the low-amplitude signals and fewer levels for the high-amplitude signals. This increases the SNR for small signals and can increase the overall dynamic range as compared to a PCM system with an equal number of bits and a uniform quantizer.

The advantage of nonuniform quantization is an increase in dynamic range for a given number of bits; this results in reduced transmission bandwidth and storage capacity for digital data and a more economical converter implementation. The disadvantage of nonuniform quantization is that quantization noise is correlated with signal amplitude, typically increasing with larger signals. Smith (1957) and Jayant (1964) have discussed the applications for speech data. Moorer (1979) has dealt with a class of nonuniform quantizers as applied to music. The most common schemes are described briefly in the next two sections.

A-law, μ-law PCM. The μ-law encoding system is commonly used for speech. This system, developed by Smith (1957), has a quantizer with a nonuniform step size that increases logarithmically for increasing levels. If the quantizer range is normalized to the interval $[-1, 1]$, the μ-law is given by

$$F(x) = \text{sgn}(x) \frac{\ln(1 + \mu|x|)}{\ln(1 + \mu)},$$

where x corresponds to the input signal, $\text{sgn}(x)$ is the sign (plus or minus) of x, $F(x)$ the μ-law compressed signal, and μ the constant determining the compression ratio. Figure 1.4 shows the μ-law transfer function for several values of μ. The most widely used application is the so-called Bell μ-255 standard with μ having a value of 255. An 8-bit μ-255 encoder achieves a small signal SNR and a total dynamic range equivalent to a 12-bit standard PCM encoder; this represents an increase of 4 bits, or 24 dB over a straight 8-bit PCM encoder.

Another logarithmically varying quantizer is described by the A-law, which is

$$F(x) = \text{sgn}(x) \frac{1 + \ln(A|x|)}{1 + \ln A} \qquad \frac{1}{A} < |x| \leq 1$$

$$= \text{sgn}(x) \frac{A|x|}{1 + \ln A} \qquad 0 \leq |x| \leq \frac{1}{A}$$

where the parameter A determines the dynamic range. This is the CCITT standard compression law.

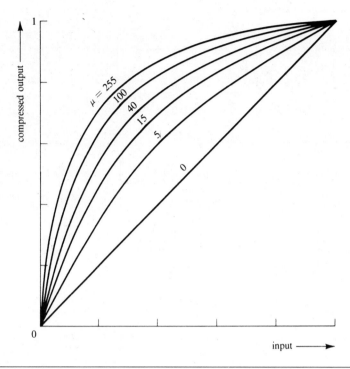

Fig. 1.4.   Transfer function of a μ-law converter for several values of μ

One caveat is worth noting with regard to μ-law and A-law. Both laws are nonlinear and therefore their effect must be undone before attempting any digital processing on signals encoded by μ-law or A-law converters.

Floating-Point PCM. Floating-point PCM (FPPCM), like μ-law and A-law, is a conversion technique that employs a nonuniform quantizer. The incoming signal is scaled prior to quantization with a scaling factor dependent upon signal level. This scaling process effectively makes the density of quantization levels vary with signal amplitude, since the density is different for each scale state. The encoded quantizer value becomes the mantissa and the scale value becomes the exponent, forming a floating-point code word.

Figure 1.5 shows block diagrams of a typical floating-point encoder and decoder. The input signal is buffered, filtered, and sampled by a sample-hold amplifier. A scale detector computes the range and exponent of a sampled signal and sets the scaler to an appropriate state. An M-bit ADC converts the scaled signal. Some converters include a syllabic time constant circuit as

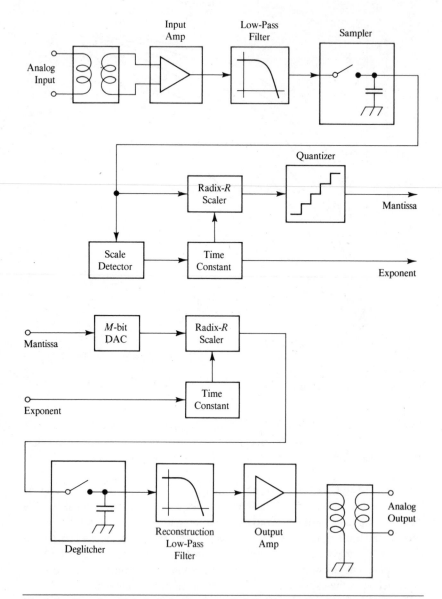

Fig. 1.5. Functional block diagram of a typical floating-point encoder and decoder

shown. This circuit causes the system to scale up instantly but scale down over some time period referred to as the *syllabic time constant*. Acceptable time constants are in the range of 5 to 20 msec (Bell Telephone Laboratories 1971, p. 678).

The dynamic range of a floating-point system is given by

$$\text{Dynamic range (dB)} \cong 6M + 20(K - 1)\log_{10} R + 1, \qquad (1.2)$$

where M is the number of bits in the mantissa, K is the number of scale states, and R is the radix of the scaler.

It is clear from equation 1.2 that FPPCM results in an increased dynamic range over a standard PCM system. The SNR of the FPPCM system, however, is not equal to the dynamic range as it is for the PCM system. It is given approximately by $6M$, where M is the number of bits in the mantissa. Graphs of the exact SNR as a function of signal level are given in several papers (e.g., Talambiras 1977).

FPPCM, especially with $R > 2$, can cause a type of distortion similar to transient-intermodulation distortion in analog circuits. Consider a signal comprised of a large-amplitude low-frequency signal and a small high-frequency signal. Specifically, assume the small signal has an amplitude of 8 and assume the radix of the scaler is 8 (a value used in some digital recording systems based on video tape recorders). Now if the low-frequency signal is large enough in amplitude to cause a scale transition, the high-frequency signal will completely disappear every time the system scales up and reappear when it scales down. The author refers to this mechanism as *scale-modulation distortion*.

Noise and Distortion in PCM

The data conversion process generates noise and distortion artifacts that degrade the original signal. Some of the degradation results from actual theoretical limitations inherent in the conversion process itself, and some results from nonideal components used in the implementation of the conversion system. Both types of degradation mechanisms are discussed briefly below. For more detailed analysis see articles by Jayant (1976), Talambiras (1976, 1985), and Blesser (1978).

An ideal PCM system with distortionless amplifiers and filters and a perfect sampler and quantizer is not noise-free. The quantizer must approximate every signal sample and thereby introduce *quantization error*. This phenomenon is described above. For a very coarse quantization, which occurs for low-level

14 JAMES F. MCGILL

signals, the quantization noise is correlated with the signal and equation 1.1 is no longer valid. Blesser (1978) has discussed this case in some detail.

The use of *dither* (i.e., additive noise) on the input signal reduces correlation between signal and noise (Roberts 1962; Schuchman 1962; Vanderkooy and Lipshitz 1984). Croll (1970) implies that dither is worth the equivalent of two extra bits in terms of reducing perceived noise. Blesser (1978) states that an adequate dither signal causes the system SNR to increase about 1.5 dB over the theoretical quantization noise limit. Dither of digitized speech signals has been studied extensively (Jayant and Rabiner 1972).

If the PCM system components are nonideal, several distortion mechanisms can be introduced, some of which will be discussed here. Talambiras (1985) has compiled a fairly complete list. Blesser (1978) has also considered these issues in some detail.

Sample Jitter. If the sample time jitters randomly with a gaussian distribution of half width t seconds, the effect is

$$\text{SNR}_t(\text{dB}) = -20\log_{10}(2\pi ft),$$

where SNR_t is the signal-to-noise ratio for a signal of frequency f Hz due to the timing jitter. For example, a 100 dB SNR_t at 1 kHz requires $t < 1.6$ nsec. The same SNR_t at 10 kHz requires $t < 0.16$ nsec.

Sample Aperture. The effect of a finite-width sample aperture has been analyzed by Zuch (1980). For a sinusoidal input signal of frequency f, the aperture time t_A given by

$$t_A = \frac{1}{2\pi f \cdot 2^M}$$

will result in a one-half-bit sampling error for an M-bit quantizer. For example, a 1 kHz signal and a 16-bit converter imply $t_A < 2.4$ ns for less than one-half bit of error.

Idle Channel Noise. The effect of noise at the quantizer input has been analyzed exhaustively by Gordon (1977).

Imperfect Quantizer. The noise contribution of imperfections in the quantizer transfer function (i.e., the transfer function is not a perfect staircase) has been analyzed by several authors (see Gordon 1977).

Imperfect DAC. Freeman (1977), Blesser (1978), and Talambiras (1985) have analyzed the imperfect digital-to-analog converter.

Filters

Typical digital recording systems include several different filters as analog processing elements. Each of these filters serves to optimize some particular aspect of the digitization process and, to the extent that it is not perfect, each one is a potential cause of signal degradation. The most common filters are discussed here. Also, a section is included on specifying and designing low-pass filters.

Input Low-pass Filter. The function of the input low-pass filter is to remove all spectral components of the input signal above one-half the sampling frequency (referred to as the *Nyquist frequency*). If energy is present above the Nyquist frequency, the sampling theorem does not hold and the sampling process folds all energy above the Nyquist frequency down into the baseband from 0 Hz to the Nyquist frequency. This distortion mechanism is called *aliasing*, because, after sampling, a baseband signal of frequency f cannot be distinguished from higher-frequency signals with frequencies $Nf_s \pm f$, where f_s is the sampling frequency and N is an integer. The input low-pass filter prevents aliasing and is therefore sometimes referred to as an *anti-aliasing filter*. The spectral consequences of aliasing are illustrated in figure 1.6.

Output Reconstruction Filter. The sampling process can be viewed mathematically as the time-domain multiplication of a signal by a string of impulses (comb function) separated in time by $T_s = 1/f_s$, where f_s is the sampling frequency. Multiplication in the time domain corresponds to convolution in the frequency domain, so the spectrum of the sampled signal is equal to the spectrum of the original signal convolved with the spectrum of the comb function. The comb function has the interesting property that its spectrum is also a comb function (the gaussian is the only other function the author knows of that has this property). The convolution of the original signal spectrum with the comb spectrum therefore yields a set of copies of the original spectrum centered about the frequencies $\pm Nf_s$, where N is an integer and f_s is the sample frequency. This spectrum is shown in figure 1.7. The copy centered about 0 Hz is identical to the original signal spectrum, and all copies centered at nonzero frequencies are artifacts of the sampling process.

When a digitized signal is converted back to analog by a digital-to-analog converter, the resulting analog signal is a sampled representation of the original signal. To make it identical to the original, it must be low-pass filtered to remove all high-frequency copies of the baseband spectrum. This output low-pass filter should cut off very sharply at the Nyquist frequency. The effectiveness of this filter is especially important for low sampling frequencies such as those used in speech recording because the higher-frequency copies of the baseband

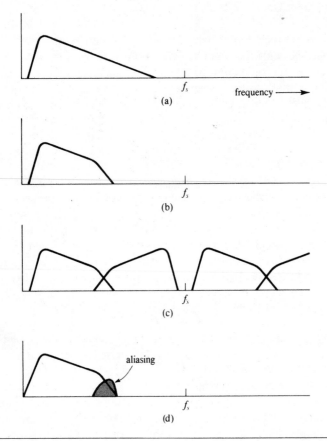

Fig. 1.6. Spectral effects of aliasing. (a) Original signal spectrum. (b) Band-limited signal spectrum. (c) Sampled signal spectrum. (d) Reconstructed signal spectrum.

spectrum may be audible. For professional-quality music recording systems, on the other hand, the Nyquist frequency is around 20 kHz, so the higher-frequency spectral copies are not audible. A filter is still required, however, to prevent these high frequencies from interacting with the bias frequency of an analog tape recorder, the sample frequency of a subsequent digital recording system, or the slew rate and overload capabilities of analog electronics.

Equalizer ($x/\sin(x)$). An ideal digital-to-analog converter outputs a sequence of impulses separated in time by the sample period. Each impulse has the amplitude of the desired analog waveform at a particular instant of time. If this sequence of impulses is low-pass filtered by an ideal filter with a cutoff at the Nyquist frequency, an ideal output waveform results. Most digital-to-analog converters deviate from ideal in that each output impulse has a finite time duration, rather than being instantaneous. If the impulse duration is constant, say T_b, then the resulting output sequence is the convolution of a single, unit-amplitude impulse of width T_b with the ideal sequence of instantaneous impulses. Therefore, the spectrum effect of the finite-width pulses is that the spectrum of the original ideal sequence is multiplied by the spectrum of the single finite-width pulse. The spectrum of the finite-width pulse is given by

$$H(\omega) = e^{-j\omega T_b/2} \left(\frac{T_b}{T_s}\right) \frac{\sin (\omega T_b/2)}{\omega T_b/2} ,$$

where ω is the angular frequency, $j^2 = -1$, and T_s is the sample period. It is common for T_s to equal T_b; in other words, the output impulse value for a particular sample is held for the entire sample period. For this case, the impulse broadening results in a 3.9 dB spectrum rolloff at the Nyquist frequency (Blesser 1978). This rolloff is of the form $\sin(x)/x$, where $x = \omega T/2$ (as shown above,

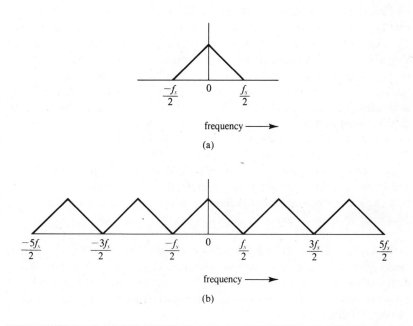

Fig. 1.7.   Sampled signal spectra. (a) Spectrum of band-limited signal. (b) Spectrum of sampled, band-limited signal, showing replication centered about the frequencies $\pm N f_s$.

with $T_b = T_s$). A filter that corrects for this rolloff has an inverse, or $x/\sin(x)$, amplitude characteristic up to the Nyquist frequency.

The $\sin(x)/x$ function rolls off at less than 6 dB/octave below the Nyquist frequency so it cannot be exactly equalized with a single zero. Blesser (1978) has considered some possible correction schemes. In general, filters that roll off at less than 6 dB/octave are called *attenuation equalizers;* Geffe (1963) has an excellent introductory discussion of such filters.

Antislewing Filter. Talambiras (1976) has shown that DAC amplifier slew-rate limiting causes signal distortion which can be several percent for slew rates on the order of 10 V/ns. Blesser (1978) calculates a slew rate of 5 V/ns to keep slew-related distortion components 100 dB down from full scale in a ± 10 V, 50 kHz sample rate system. To avoid slewing, a single-pole low-pass filter is typically placed on the digital-to-analog converter output. If this filter has too low a cutoff frequency, it attenuates baseband signals. On the other hand, it must be slow enough to prevent slewing. Amplifiers with slew rates of 10 mV/ns are readily available; for a ± 10 V system, this value translates to a maximum frequency of about 160 kHz for a full-scale sine wave without slewing (i.e., the maximum slope of the sine wave must be less than the slew rate limit). A single-pole filter with $\tau = 1$ μs has a -3 dB point at about 160 kHz, so it should never allow a full-scale 160 kHz signal and therefore should satisfy the requirement to prevent slewing. However, things are actually twice as bad as they seem. In a ± 10 V system the largest possible digital-to-analog converter output signal is a 20 V step (from -10 V to $+10$ V). If this step is applied to the input of a single-pole filter with $\tau = 1$ μs, the filter output signal is an exponential with a 1 μs time constant and an initial slope of 20 mV/ns, which exceeds the slew rate by a factor of 2. Therefore, the time constant for the antislewing filter must be at least 2 μs for the assumed system. This value corresponds to a -3 dB point of 80 kHz. Notice that if the antislewing amplifier has a time constant of 8 μs or more, the amplitude attenuation effects may require compensation in the audio band (i.e., an 8 μs filter has a -3 dB frequency of about 20 kHz).

Deglitching Filter. Digital-to-analog converters have large switching transients (glitches) when responding to a changing digital input. In a high-quality system, these must be blocked by a deglitching amplifier which either switches to ground or holds the previous sample value during an update of the digital-to-analog converter.

For the reasons described earlier, this amplifier must not slew limit as it acquires a new value. A common solution is a sample-hold amplifier with exponential acquisition which prevents slewing by causing a rolloff of high frequencies.

The frequency dependence of the amplitude response is given by

$$H(s) = \frac{1 - e^{-sT}}{sT} \frac{1}{1 + sT_{RC}} \frac{1 - Ke^{-sT_b}}{1 - Ke^{-sT}},$$

where T_{RC} is the sample acquisition time constant, $K = \exp(-T_b/T_{RC})$, $s = j\omega$, and T_b is the total sample acquisition time. (Blesser [1978] has given a very elegant derivation of this result, but he omitted the $1/T$ normalization factor.) The first term of the product is that of an ideal sample-hold amplifier with infinite slew rate; the second term is a single-pole low-pass filter with -3 dB frequency of $1/(2\pi T_{RC})$, and the third term accounts for the ratios of the three time intervals (T, T_b, and T_{RC}). For example, a system with 50 kHz sample frequency ($T = 20\,\mu s$), $T_{RC} = 2\,\mu s$, and $T_b = 10\,\mu s$ has an amplitude attenuation of -2.8 dB at 20 kHz due to the deglitching amplifier.

It should be noted that when a deglitching amplifier is used, the $\sin(x)/x$ spectral effect described in the previous section is superseded by the spectral effect of the deglitching amplifier. Notice, however, that the deglitching amplifier response given above can be rewritten

$$H(s) = e^{-sT/2} \frac{\sin(\omega T/2)}{\omega T/2} \frac{1}{1 + sT_{RC}} \frac{1 - Ke^{-sT_b}}{1 - Ke^{-sT}},$$

so the $\sin(x)/x$ effect is embedded in this response function.

Specifying Low-Pass Filters. A low-pass filter passes signals of frequency less than the *cutoff frequency* and attenuates higher-frequency signals. Frequencies that pass comprise the *passband;* those that are attenuated make up the *stopband.*

A filter is characterized by its *transfer function,* which expresses (as a function of frequency) the effect of the filter on the amplitude and phase of a signal. It can be shown (Lam 1979) that the transfer function of a filter built from a finite number of standard components (i.e., resistors, capacitors, inductors, transformers, and active devices) must be a rational function of the variable $s = j\omega$, where $j = \sqrt{-1}$ and ω is the angular frequency in radians/sec. That is,

$$H(s) = \frac{1 + \sum_{i=1}^{M} a_i s^i}{\sum_{i=0}^{N} b_i s^i},$$

where $H(s)$ is the transfer function and the values M and N increase with the number of components in the filter.

Notice that only $N + M + 1$ parameters are used to totally specify $H(s)$. This means that an arbitrary filter response function can only be approximated by an actual transfer function of the form $H(s)$. For example, figure 1.8 shows an ideal low-pass-filter transfer function and an example of a realizable approximation.

The two fundamental problems of filter design are, given a transfer-function specification, to find an optimal *approximation* in the form of $H(s)$ and to convert that polynomial equation to a *realization* by finding the actual component values for a given circuit morphology. Some filter approximations have

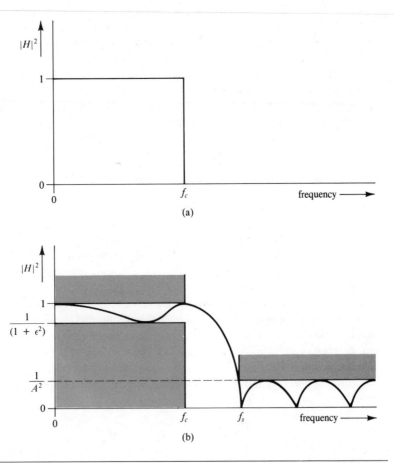

Fig. 1.8. Frequency responses of low-pass filters. (a) Ideal low-pass filter. (b) Realizable elliptic low-pass filter.

been found to be consistently useful and, as a result, their characteristics have been tabulated in the literature. These common approximations (Lam 1979) are:

1. The *Butterworth* filter, characterized by a monotonically decreasing amplitude function of ω for $\omega \geq 0$.
2. The *Chebyshev* filter, characterized by an equiripple amplitude response in the passband and a monotonically decreasing amplitude response in the stopband.
3. The *inverse Chebyshev* filter, characterized by a monotonically decreasing amplitude response in the passband and an equiripple response in the stopband.
4. The *elliptic* or *Cauer* filter, characterized by equiripple response in both the passband and the stopband and by the steepest transition rate for a given order of realization.
5. The *Bessel* filter, characterized as having an optimally linear phase response.

There exist analytic techniques for approximating and realizing filters, but in many cases design tables and graphs are used instead. Orchard and Temes (1968) provide an excellent annotated index into what they refer to as "instant design information." Gray and Markel (1976) provide a list of references for elliptic filter design, and Saal and Ulbrich (1958) and Christian and Eisenmann (1966) still remain as seminal references in the field.

Input and output low-pass filters for digital recording systems require a very steep rolloff at the band edge to minimize aliasing while at the same time allowing the sample frequency to be as low as possible. Because of these constraints, the elliptic filter is the appropriate choice. An elliptic filter is specified by the amplitude of *passband ripple,* the *minimum stopband attenuation,* the *cutoff ratio* (f_s/f_c in figure 1.8) and the *order* of the realization. These parameters are related (Gray and Markel 1976) by

$$ N = \frac{2}{\pi^2} \ln\left(\frac{4A}{\epsilon}\right) \ln\left(\frac{8}{2\pi \frac{f_s}{f_c} - 1}\right), $$

where N is the filter order and A, ϵ, f_c, and f_s are shown in figure 1.8. This formula allows one to estimate the order of a filter required to meet a given filter performance specification.

Circuit designs for elliptic low-pass filters for digital recording applications have been published by Matthews et al. (1969), Doi et al. (1978), Muraoka et al. (1978), and Lagadec et al. (1980). Figure 1.9 shows the circuit diagram of an

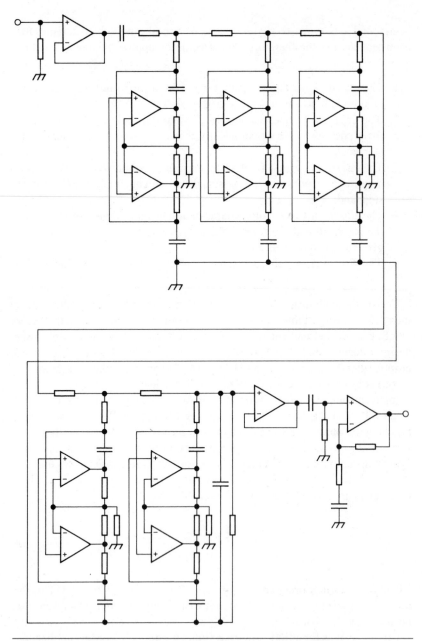

Fig. 1.9. Circuit diagram of an eleventh-order elliptic low-pass filter

eleventh-order elliptic filter designed by the author for use in a 16-bit digital recording system. The filter was designed using current techniques for realization with active devices (Bruton 1969; Dubois and Neirynck 1977). The circuit achieves a rolloff rate of 360 dB/octave at the band edge with stopband attenuation of 90 dB and passband ripple of 0.5 dB.

Sample Frequency

There are several issues in the selection of a sample frequency. Foremost is the requirement that the sample frequency f_s be at least two times the highest signal frequency of interest, and in practical applications this ratio should be about 2.5 to avoid foldover in the filter transition band. A low sample frequency is desirable to minimize the digital transmission bandwidth and the total amount of digital storage medium required, and a high sample frequency is desired for signal fidelity. For a professional-quality system, an audio bandwidth of 20 kHz is required, which implies a sample frequency in the neighborhood of 50 kHz.

Several standard sample frequencies are used in commercially available digitizing equipment. The North American and European telephone networks support both analog and digital data. The digital data is sampled at 8 kHz. The Audio Engineering Society has recommended 48 kHz for professional recording studio applications and 32 kHz for broadcast and transmission-related applications (Audio Engineering Society 1984). There are consumer products available for adapting 1/2-inch video tape recorders to record digital audio. These devices sample at 44.1 kHz in order to synchronize the audio samples with video framing formats. Finally, Digital Sound Corporation manufactures a digitizing device for speech research laboratories (the DSC-200) that allows sample rate selection in 1/4 μs steps from 20 μs to 16 ms.

Sample Rate Translation. Translation between different sample rates is a process which is important to consider. For example, suppose a segment of music has been recorded into digital memory (or synthesized there) at a certain sample rate. This segment may be transferred to a digital tape recorder by converting to analog and back to digital again, or it may be done entirely in the digital domain. Reconverting the data will add about 6 dB of noise (assuming the existing noise floor was comparable in magnitude to the quantization noise and that the DAC and ADC quantization errors are comparable and uncorrelated). A direct digital transfer has no associated degradation if the original sample rate is the same as the destination sample rate. For the case of differing sample rates, computational algorithms exist for performing the translation (Crochiere and Rabiner 1975, 1981, 1983; Yamasaki and Sugawara 1978; Lagadec and Kunz

1981; Lagadec 1983; Rabiner 1983; Ramstad 1984; Smith and Gossett 1984). It turns out to be a relatively simple process for the case of the two sample rates having a ratio which is equal to the ratio of two integers. Furthermore, smaller integers result in less computation. The noise contribution of the arithmetic, if done properly, should be no more than 3 dB.

Coding for Data Compression

The *bit rate,* or number of bits per second, is an important design parameter for any digital recording system. From it derive the transmission bandwidth, storage capacity, computational rate requirements, and therefore, the cost of system hardware. A lower bit rate results in lower hardware cost, but bit reduction is usually accomplished at the expense of signal fidelity.

Moorer (1979) has investigated Huffman coding and floating-point coding as potential compression schemes. Huffman coding relies on the assumption that the amplitude values of the waveform to be coded are not uniformly distributed. This being the case, short codes are assigned to frequently occurring amplitude values, and longer codes to less frequently occurring values. One of the principal advantages of this scheme is that no information is lost, so the data compression comes with no degradation of data quality. However, the compression is only efficient if the waveform amplitude distribution is well matched by the codes. A mismatch (i.e., assigning the longer codes to the more frequent amplitude values) can actually result in an increase in data rate over straight PCM encoding. Another potential disadvantage of Huffman coding is that a fixed amount of data may contain a varying number of samples.

A type of floating-point coding (FPPCM) has already been discussed in this chapter. Moorer (1979) covers a more general class of floating-point codes and concludes that floating-point incremental coders can yield significant bit reduction. The disadvantages are that signal fidelity is compromised in the compression process (by allowing an amplitude-dependent signal-to-noise ratio) and that a sample in the middle of a data clock cannot be referenced at random—the block must be read from the beginning.

Doi (1979) reports on variable-length codes, including Huffman coding experiments with digital audio. He concludes that the coding is efficient but difficult to apply on digital tape recorders because error correction is a problem with a varying number of bits per time interval.

Doi (1979) introduces what he refers to as *segment coding,* a scheme that had also been looked at by the author (McGill 1977). More generally, this is referred to as *group coding* and is used by designers of computer tape machines and disk drivers to guarantee run-length-limited (dc-free) codes for recording onto the magnetic media. To understand the technique, consider a 16-bit PCM sample encoded as sign plus magnitude. For small positive or negative amplitude values, only a few low-order bits are turned on. If the 16-bit word is broken into 4-bit segments, then only the segments with bits turned on need to be stored for a given sample. Each 4-bit segment needs an extra bit added to indicate the first segment in a sample. With this segmentation the worst case is 20 bits per sample; but the best case is 5 bits per sample, so if the most frequent amplitude values are small, there can be significant bit reduction over the initial 16 bits per sample. Doi (1979) reports 30 to 40 percent bit reduction from applying segment coding to a differentiated audio signal. This technique does not compromise signal quality but does result in a varying number of bits per time interval.

Probably the most successful compression scheme for digital speech data is linear predictive coding (LPC). A typical telephone-grade speech channel might have 3 kHz of bandwidth and 50 dB of SNR. Digitization at 8 bits per sample at a rate of 8 kHz yields a bit rate of 64 kb/s. The LPC technique applied to such data results in a bit rate of 2.4 kb/s, for a compression ratio of 26 : 1. The author has applied LPC in the compression of isolated musical tones (McGill 1976) with some degree of success, but no work has yet been done on polyphony. In speech applications, LPC is known to fail for signals with multiple speakers, and similar problems are to be expected for polyphonic music. LPC can result in signal degradation since information is discarded in the coding process.

CONCLUSION

This chapter has introduced some of the concepts of digital recording. Because of space and time constraints, some rather deep subjects were only briefly mentioned, and others were completely omitted. Many of these are discussed elsewhere in this volume.

REFERENCES

Audio Engineering Society. 1984. AES recommended practice for professional digital audio applications—Preferred sampling frequencies. *Journal of the Audio Engineering Society* 32(10):781–85.

Bell Telephone Laboratories Technical Staff. 1971. *Transmission systems for communications*. Winston-Salem, N. C.: Western Electric Company Technical Publications.

Bennett, W. R. 1948. Spectra of quantized signals. *Bell System Technical Journal* 27:446–72.

Blesser, Barry A. 1978. Digitization of audio. *Journal of the Audio Engineering Society* 26(10):739–71.

Bruton, L. T. 1969. Network transfer functions using the concept of frequency-dependent negative resistance. *IEEE Transactions on Circuit Theory* CT-16:406–8.

Cauchy, A. L. 1841. Mémoire sur diverses formules d'analyse. *Comptes Rendus Hebdomadaires des Séances de l'Académie des Sciences Paris,* 12:283–98.

Christian, E., and E. Eisenmann. 1966. *Filter design tables and graphs.* New York: Wiley.

Crochiere, R. E., and L. R. Rabiner. 1975. Optimum FIR digital filter implementations for decimation, interpolation and narrow-band filtering. *IEEE Proceedings on Acoustics, Speech, and Signal Processing* ASSP-2:444–56.

Crochiere, R. E., and L. R. Rabiner. 1981. Interpolation and decimation of digital signals—A tutorial review. *Proceedings of the IEEE* 69(3):300–331.

Crochiere, R. E., and L. R. Rabiner. 1983. *Multiple digital signal processing.* Englewood Cliffs, N.J.: Prentice-Hall.

Croll, M. 1970. *Pulse code modulation for high quality sound distribution: Quantizing distortion at very low signal levels.* London: BBC Research Engineering Division.

Doi, T. 1979. On bit reduction of digital audio systems. Audio Engineering Society Convention, Preprint 1549 (H-1).

Doi, T. 1980. On the sampling rate for digital audio recorders. *Journal of the Audio Engineering Society* 28:616–18.

Doi, T., Y. Tsuchiya, and A. Iga. 1978. On several standards for converting PCM signals into video signals. *Journal of the Audio Engineering Society* 26:641–49.

Dubois, D., and J. Neirynck. 1977. Synthesis of a leapfrog configuration equivalent to an LC-ladder filter between generalized terminations. *IEEE Transactions on Circuits and Systems* CAS-24:590–97.

Freeman, D. 1977. Slewing distortion in digital-to-analog conversion. *Journal of the Audio Engineering Society* 25:178–83.

Geffe, P. R. 1963. *Simplified modern filter design.* New York: John Rider.

Gilbert, E. N. 1960. Capacity of a burst-noise channel. *Bell System Technical Journal* 39:1253–65.

Gordon, B. M., ed. 1977. *The analogic data-conversion systems digest.* Norwood, Mass.: Analogic Corp.

Gray, A. H., and J. D. Markel. 1976. A computer program for designing digital elliptic filters. *IEEE Proceedings on Acoustics, Speech, and Signal Processing* ASSP-24:529–38.

Hamming, R. W. 1950. Error detecting and error correcting codes. *Bell System Technical Journal* 26:147–60.

Hartley, R. V. L. 1928. Transmission of information. *Bell System Technical Journal* 7:535–63.

Huffman, D. A. 1952. A method for the construction of minimum redundancy codes. *Proceedings of the IRE* 40:1098–1101.

Jayant, N. S. 1964. Digital coding of speech waveforms: PCM, DPCM and DM quantizers. *Proceedings of the IEEE* 62:611–32.

Jayant, N. S., ed. 1976. *Waveform quantization and coding.* New York: IEEE Press.

Jayant, N. S., and L. R. Rabiner. 1972. The application of dither to the quantization of speech signals. *Bell System Technical Journal* 51:1293–1304.

Lagadec, R. 1983. Digital sampling frequency conversion. In B. Blesser, B. Locanthi, and T. Stockham, eds. *Digital audio*. New York: Audio Engineering Society, pp. 90–98.

Lagadec, R., and H. O. Kunz. 1981. A new approach to digital sampling frequency conversion. Audio Engineering Society Convention, Preprint 1749 (D-2).

Lagadec, R., D. Weiss, and R. Greutmann. 1980. High quality analog filters for digital audio. Audio Engineering Society Convention, Preprint 1707 (B-4).

Lam, H. Y.-F. 1979. *Analog and digital filters*. Englewood Cliffs, N. J.: Prentice-Hall.

Linden, D. A. 1959. A discussion of sampling theorems. *Proceedings of the IRE* 47:1219–26.

McGill, J. F. 1976. *Music synthesis by optimal filtering*. Santa Barbara, Calif.: Culler-Harrison, Inc. Technical Note CHI-TN-76-012.

McGill, J. F. 1977. *Group coding for data compression*. Santa Barbara, Calif.: Digital Sound Corporation. Engineering Note EN-JM10.

Mathews, Max V., with Joan E. Miller, F. Richard Moore, John R. Pierce, and Jean-Claude Risset. *The technology of computer music*. Cambridge: Mass.: MIT Press, 1969.

Moorer, James A. 1979. The digital coding of high-quality musical sound. *Journal of the Audio Engineering Society* 27:657–66.

Muraoka, T., Y. Yoshihiko, and M. Yamazaki. 1978. Sampling frequency considerations in digital audio. *Journal of the Audio Engineering Society* 26:252–56.

Nakajima, Heitaro, Toshitada Doi, Jyoji Fukuda, and Akira Iga. 1983. *Dijitaru odio gijutsu nyūmon*. Translated as *Digital audio technology*. Blue Ridge Summit, Pa.: Tab Books.

Nyquist, H. 1928. Certain topics in telegraph transmission theory. *Transactions of the American Institute of Electrical Engineers* 47:617–44.

Oliver, B. M., J. R. Pierce, and C. E. Shannon. 1948. The philosophy of PCM. *Proceedings of the IRE* 36:1324–31.

Orchard, H. J., and G. C. Temes. 1968. Filter design using transformed variables. *IEEE Transactions on Circuit Theory* CT-15:385–408.

Rabiner, L. 1983. Digital techniques for changing the sampling rate of a signal. In B. Blesser, B. Locanthi, and T. Stockham, eds. *Digital audio*. New York: Audio Engineering Society, pp. 79–89.

Ramstad, T. A. 1984. Digital methods for conversion between arbitrary sampling features. *IEEE Proceedings on Acoustics, Speech, and Signal Processing* ASSP-32:577–91.

Reeves, A. H. 1938. Electric signaling system. French Patent No. 852,183. British Patent No. 535,860. U.S. Patent No. 2,272,070 (1942).

Roberts, L. 1962. Picture coding using pseudo-random noise. *IRE Transactions on Information Theory* IT-8:145–54.

Saal, R., and E. Ulbrich. 1958. On the design of filters by synthesis. *IRE Transactions on Information Theory* IT-5:284–327.

Schuchman, L. 1962. Dither signals and their effect on quantization. *IEEE Transactions on Communications Theory* COM-12:162–65.

Shannon, C. E. 1948. A mathematical theory of communication. *Bell System Technical Journal* 27:379–423, 623–56.

Smith, B. 1957. Instantaneous companding of quantized signals. *Bell System Technical Journal* 36:653–709.

Smith, J., and P. Gossett. 1984. A flexible sample-rate conversion method. *Proceedings of the IEEE Conference on Acoustics, Speech, and Signal Processing* 2:19.4.1–19.4.2, San Diego, Calif.: March 1984.

Talambiras, R. P. 1976. Digital-to-analog converters: Some problems in producing high fidelity signals. *Computer Design* 15:63–69.

Talambiras, R. P. 1977. Some considerations in the design of wide-dynamic-range audio digitizing systems. Audio Engineering Society Convention, Preprint 1226 (A-1).

Talambiras, R. P. 1985. Limitations on the dynamic range of digitized audio. In John Strawn, ed. *Digital audio engineering: An anthology*. Los Altos, Calif.: Kaufmann.

Vanderkooy, J., and S. P. Lipshitz. 1984. Resolution below the least significant bit in digital systems with dither. *Journal of the Audio Engineering Society* 32:106–13.

Yamasaki, Y., and H. Sugawara. 1978. Design of a real-time sampling rate conversion system. Audio Engineering Society Convention, Preprint 1427 (H-2).

Zuch, E. L. 1980. Graphs give aperture time required for A-D conversion. In Zuch, E. L., ed. *Data acquisition handbook*. Cupertino, Calif.: Intersil, pp. 148–51.

2

LIMITATIONS ON THE DYNAMIC RANGE OF DIGITIZED AUDIO

Robert Talambiras

With the advent of high-speed multitrack digital recorders and consumer video recorders, it has become economically and technically feasible to think about using digital recording techniques both in the professional recording and broadcasting industries, and in the final consumer market (Warnock 1976; Blesser et al. 1983; Nakajima et al. 1983). In the recording of music, nondegradable masters can be made which have many advantages. The consumer can expect superior performance in terms of wide dynamic range and low distortion, the properties of digitizing systems with which this discussion is concerned.

Portions of this article appeared previously in Talambiras (1976) and Talambiras (1977).

DYNAMIC RANGE

Lee and Lipschutz (1977) discuss the dynamic range requirements for ideal recording. Briefly, a recording studio may have a background sound pressure level (SPL) of 20 dB and a symphony orchestra may peak at about 120 dB, giving a dynamic range of 100 dB. Rock music may exceed the threshold of pain (130 dB), but then a little clipping may not be noticeable. Olson (1947) gives the average noise (A-weighted) of a residence as 43 SPL, and one's neighbors may set the upper level at less than 120 SPL, so that a 100 dB dynamic range is quite conservative. On the other hand, one could possibly come close to a full range using earphones in a quiet room. Kozinn (1980) points out that some listeners with "hybrid" recordings (digital master, analog disk) are already complaining that the increased dynamic range is blasting their speakers!

In discussing dynamic range and distortion we shall refer to the systems in figure 2.1. The input voltage from the microphone amplifier is passed through an anti-aliasing low-pass filter, amplified if necessary, and converted to a digital code in an analog-to-digital (A/D) converter. On playback from the digital recording medium, the digital code is converted to a voltage in the digital-to-analog (D/A) converter, deglitched in the sample-and-hold (or strobed amplifier), low-pass filtered, and then amplified to a suitable power level for the

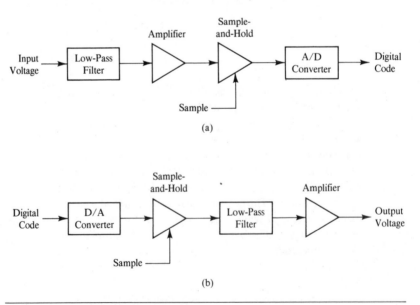

Fig. 2.1.   Simple A/D and D/A systems

audio system. A more economically practical system is shown in figure 2.2 in which each converter handles two channels of audio. The discussion is applicable to either system.

The fundamental limitation on the dynamic range of the system of figure 2.1 is set by the A/D converter. A section of the input-output characteristic of an ideal A/D converter is shown in figure 2.3a where q is taken to be the amplitude of one least significant bit (LSB). The difference in transfer function between the actual converter and one with an infinitely small LSB is the quantizing error

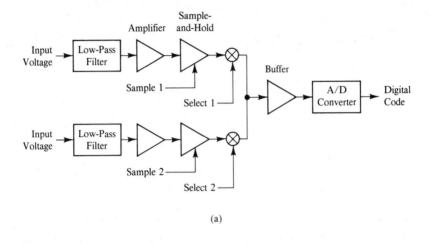

(a)

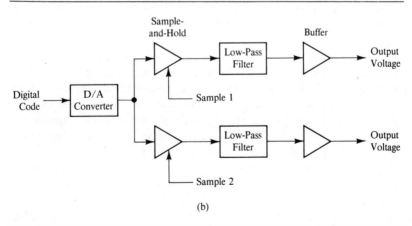

(b)

Fig. 2.2. Two-channel A/D and D/A systems incorporating only one converter in each direction

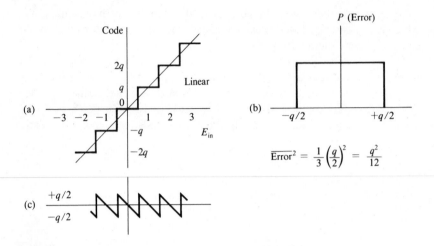

Fig. 2.3. (a) Output vs input for an A/D converter, where q is the amplitude of the least significant bit. (b) Error probability distribution. (c) Quantizing error.

shown in figure 2.3c, which varies between $\pm q/2$. Generation of the quantizing noise can be explained if we imagine the characteristic in figure 2.3a to be a transfer function with the input on the horizontal axis and the output on the vertical axis. Bennett (1948) has shown that for inputs of reasonable size (more than a few LSB), the sawtooth transfer function does such a good job of chopping up the input that there is essentially zero correlation between the input and the error voltage (quantizing noise). The error voltage can therefore be treated as an independent noise source, although, to be sure, it requires a signal to generate it. With a very small signal such as a decaying piano tone, very good A/D and D/A converters with low noise, a pair of headphones in a quiet room, and a golden ear, one can hear the correlation between the noise and the signal. However, for all practical systems, the independent noise source is an excellent approximation for the quantizing error voltage. (Blesser [1978] discusses the case of very low signal levels, where the quantizing error must be looked at in terms of distortion rather than uncorrelated noise.)

The approximation is equivalent to saying that the error is uniformly distributed between $+q/2$ and $-q/2$ as shown in figure 2.3b, and therefore the mean square value of the error voltage is $q^2/12$. The rms noise is then just $q/\sqrt{12}$. The quantizing noise is wideband, usually many times the system sampling frequency. Bennett (1956) has also shown that the net effect of sampling wideband noise is equivalent to sampling noise with the same rms value which had been band-limited to one-half the sampling frequency (often called the Nyquist frequency). The noise power in our audio output will therefore be

$$P_N = \frac{q^2}{12} \frac{F_B}{F_{Ny}} , \qquad (2.1)$$

where F_B is the equivalent noise bandwidth of the low-pass output filter and F_{Ny} is the Nyquist frequency. For the kind of filters used in these systems the equivalent noise bandwidth F_B can be assumed to be the 3 dB down frequency.

We define the maximum signal power (P_S) as the power in a sine wave that goes exactly from plus full scale to minus full scale. Therefore, in a converter with n bits (including sign), the maximum signal power is

$$P_S = \frac{(2^{n-1})^2 q^2}{2}$$

$$= q^2 2^{(2n-3)} . \qquad (2.2)$$

With the noise power given in equation 2.1, the maximum power signal-to-noise ratio is

$$\left(\frac{S}{N}\right)_P = 1.5 \frac{F_{Ny} \, 2^{2n}}{F_B} . \qquad (2.3)$$

In dB, the maximum S/N ratio, which we define as the dynamic range, is

$$\text{dynamic range} = \left[(1.76 + 6.02n) + 10 \log_{10} \left(\frac{F_{Ny}}{F_B}\right) \right] \text{dB.} \qquad (2.4)$$

Table 2.1 gives the dynamic range for different numbers of bits in the converter, and table 2.2 gives the number of dB to add to the dynamic range as a function of F_B/F_{Ny}. Note that table 2.1 gives the maximum dynamic range achievable with an ideal converter. Any practical system will have additional sources of noise that will reduce the dynamic range from the values given in table 2.1.

Before discussing the imperfections of practical converters, some system limitations to dynamic range should be pointed out. If the output of the A/D converter is simply recorded and then played back into a D/A converter, no quantizing noise is introduced in the playback process. If, however, the digitized signal is first processed in a digital mixdown console, we must add one more quantizing noise power (eq. 2.1) to the system noise. If attenuation (multiplication) is done in the console, then even if extra bits are carried to avoid significant roundoff error in the console, we must still round off the result to the number of bits in the D/A converter. The resulting roundoff noise is identical to the A/D quantizing noise and, since it is uncorrelated with it, adds 3 dB to the noise power. Therefore, the ideal system dynamic range with a digital mixdown

TABLE 2.1   Dynamic range as a function of the number of bits n in the D/A converter, as given by the $(1.76 + 6.02n)$ term of equation 2.4

n	Dynamic Range (dB)
17	104.10
16	98.08
15	92.06
14	86.04
13	80.02
12	74.00
11	67.98
10	61.96
9	55.94

console (or any other digital processing that is not simply fixed-point addition or subtraction with no guard bits) will be 3 dB less than the figures in table 2.1.

At the upper end of the dynamic range we must allow for the ratio of peak to rms power known as *headroom* in the audio industry and *crest factor* in the instrumentation field. The numbers in table 2.1 were calculated for a sine wave which has a crest factor of 3 dB. It is common to allow 12 dB of headroom for music, where the rms value is a short-term measurement such as one might obtain with a VU meter. We must therefore subtract 9 dB from the dynamic range in table 2.1 for music signals. (Note that "dynamic range" is not a standardized term. We use it as the ratio of rms signal to rms noise. Some workers use it to refer to the ratio of peak signal to rms noise, and some use it for the

TABLE 2.2   Effect of equivalent noise bandwidth of low-pass filter on the dynamic range

F_B/F_{Ny}	Add (dB)
1.0	0.00
0.9	0.46
0.8	0.97
0.7	1.55
0.6	2.22
0.5	3.01

Note: The figures in the right-hand column as given by the $10 \log_{10} (F_B/F_{Ny})$ term in equation 2.4 are to be added to the numbers in Table 2.1.

ratio of peak signal to peak noise.) Therefore, if 12 dB headroom is used, and the signal is digitally processed, the dynamic range of an ideal system can be as much as 12 dB less than the numbers in table 2.1.

DYNAMIC RANGE AND DISTORTION IN PRACTICAL SYSTEMS

In systems such as those shown in figure 2.1, there are many sources of *idle* noise and *dynamic* noise. Idle noise is used in the communications industry to denote the noise when there is no signal present. With digitizing systems we extend the definition to include the noise present when there is a small input so that the quantizing noise is excited. Dynamic noise denotes the noise generated with large input signals, and is caused by distortion in the various links in the communications chain. It is equivalent to the total distortion specifications in the audio industry. In communications, random noise is often used as a test signal, whereas in audio, sine waves are the common test signal. Neither one is a good approximation to music, but we can write specifications in terms of these signals which we can't do with music.

Table 2.3 is a list of sources of error in the systems of figure 2.1, with each source classified as idle or dynamic. The division is not always clear-cut since converter errors can fall into either category depending on whether they exist around 0 or not. If table 2.3 looks imposing, it is meant to be, since there seems to be an unfortunate tendency on the part of potential users to use the theoretical S/N numbers as a system specification, ignoring the practical limitations of actual systems.

If we total the error sources, we find 11 idle noise sources and 18 dynamic noise sources. They are not all equally important, but on a first pass it is reasonable to assign them equal value. We saw initially that it would be desirable to keep the idle noise to 100 dB below maximum signals, but this ratio does not seem practical to achieve with a 16-bit system, since limited experience indicates an actual idle noise of between 6 to 10 dB above quantizing noise. Lee and Lipschutz (1977) indicate that if the dynamic noise can be kept 70 dB below the signal level, it will be masked by the signal. A 70 dB dynamic signal-to-noise ratio appears to be a reasonable and conservative goal, since their testing was done on an A-B comparison basis which we can expect to be more severe than tests done on a "perceptible," "tolerable," or "objectionable" type of subjective evaluation.

It is convenient when working with A/D converters to define a 0 dB reference for a full-scale-to-full-scale sine wave. The quantizing noise in the Nyquist bandwidth for a 16-bit converter would then be -98.08 dB FS (table 2.1). There is

TABLE 2.3   Idle and dynamic sources of noise in the systems shown in figure 2.1

Noise Source	Idle	Dynamic
Nonlinearity in the filters caused by the inductors in a passive filter or by the amplifiers in an active filter		X
Input amplifier		
Noise	X	
Static nonlinearity		X
Dynamic nonlinearity (slew-limiting)		X
Sample and hold		
Noise	X	
Static nonlinearity		X
Dynamic nonlinearity		X
Sampling jitter		X
Feedthrough from input when in HOLD		X
A/D converter		
Quantizing noise	X	
Noise in the comparator and on the references	X	
Nonuniform code widths	X	X
D/A converter		
Nonuniform code widths	X	X
Noise on the references	X	
Output sample and hold		
Noise	X	
Static nonlinearity		X
Dynamic nonlinearity		X
Sampling jitter		X
Feedthrough from input when in HOLD	X	X
Modulation of glitches		X
Output amplifier		
Noise	X	
Static nonlinearity		X
Dynamic nonlinearity		X
"Ground" noise and coupling from the digital lines	X	X
Aliasing noise		X

also a certain convenience in assuming that we have a filter at the Nyquist bandwidth and that we obtain conservative results; practical systems might have a sampling frequency on the order of 50 kHz with a filter 3 dB point at 18 kHz. There is no magic set of numbers, and the final parameters are a compromise among recorder bit rate, filter complexity, and signal bandwidth. If we assume signal bandwidth of 20 kHz, a 16-bit converter, an idle noise (that includes quantizing noise) of 8 dB above quantizing noise, and 11 independent noise sources, we can assign numbers to some of the noise sources that make up the idle noise. The quantizing noise in the Nyquist bandwidth is − 98.08 dB FS. We add 8 dB to this value to get the practical idle noise of − 90.08 dB FS. Since 11 sources are assumed to contribute equal noise, we subtract $10 \log 11 = 10.41$ dB FS to get the allowable noise contribution per source of − 100.5 dB FS. Since this level is below the quantizing noise level, we reallocate quantizing noise to be − 98.08 dB FS and it follows that the other sources must be at − 100.83 dB FS. We round off the noise allowed to − 100 dB FS in the following calculations.

IDLE NOISE SOURCES

For calculating the various allowed noise sources, we shall assume an A/D converter with ± 10 V FS and a sine-wave signal. For signals with other crest factors, the allowable noise can be scaled accordingly, depending on one's definition of dynamic range.

The full-scale output of the input amplifier is 7.07 V rms. If we assume an equivalent noise bandwidth of 100 kHz for the input amplifier, the output noise density must be less than 224 nV/$\sqrt{\text{Hz}}$ for the amplifier noise to be − 100 dB FS. If we assume an average IC operational amplifier with an input noise density of 20 nV/$\sqrt{\text{Hz}}$, then the input FS signal must be greater than 630 mV rms. Since this is less than normal audio level, the noise from the input amplifier should not be a problem.

The sample-and-hold operates at standard converter levels, which are ± 10 V for full scale. This level corresponds to a sine wave with an rms value of 7.07 V. A level of − 100 dB from this level is 70.7 μV rms. High-speed sample-and-holds generally run somewhat more than this, on the order of 90 μV rms, so we can expect the sample-and-hold to contribute somewhat more than its allocation of noise.

If we assume a 16-bit A/D converter with ± 10 V FS, the quantizing noise is 88 μV rms referred to the A/D input, and one LSB is 305 μV. Calculations and experience indicate that we can expect a total equivalent input noise from the A/D converter (i.e., from the comparator, resistors, and references) on the order of 30 μV rms or − 107.5 dB FS (exclusive of quantizing noise).

The D/A converter must have a bandwidth in its amplifier and in the sample-and-hold only slightly less than the input sample-and-hold to the A/D converter because of settling time requirements; and since this noise is inside a sampling system, it all gets beaten down into the Nyquist bandwidth. Therefore, the (implied) amplifier in the D/A converter and the sample-and-hold contribute about as much noise as the input sample-and-hold. If the output sample-and-hold is a deglitcher holding only during the transition time of the D/A converter, or is a strobed amplifier which is grounded during the D/A transition time, there is no beating down of the noise into the Nyquist bandwidth. In this case, the output noise power from the D/A output amplifier and the deglitcher is the product of their noise power density and the bandwidth of the output filter. The final output buffer amplifier contributes about the same amount of noise as the input amplifier.

The digital code varies with the signal, and pickup of the digital signals in the analog circuitry will result in noise and distortion, since Bennett (Schwartz, Bennett, Stein 1966) has shown that the input signal, plus harmonics and beats with the sampling frequency, can be detected in the code if it is simply filtered and put through an amplifier. It is difficult to quantify this number, but the author has detected it at levels of -90 to -95 dB FS.

Perhaps the most important idle noise source, and an important dynamic noise source as well, comes from imperfections in the transfer characteristic of the A/D and D/A converters. The most common and straightforward A/D and D/A converters use unipolar switches with an offset to center the characteristic around 0 as shown in figure 2.4. (This figure will be discussed in more detail

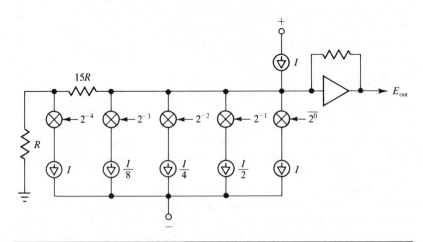

Fig. 2.4. Typical two's-complement D/A converter

below.) The major (and most critical) carry is around 0, and errors in this carry can produce noise and distortion. Figure 2.5 illustrates a D/A characteristic with an error around 0. A similar plot can be made for an A/D converter. The transfer function can be broken into a perfect transfer characteristic plus a step at 0. We can calculate the effect of the step nonlinearity for both a random and a sine wave input if we keep to our assumption that our filters are at the Nyquist bandwidth. Then *all* of the distortion is beaten into the signal band and we only have to calculate the rms value of the distortion (more accurately, we calculate the square root of the variance since we don't care about dc errors).

Let us assume that the step nonlinearity has an amplitude E. Then an input signal of reasonable amplitude will give rise to a rectangular error wave of peak-to-peak height E. For a random input or a sine-wave input, the mean square value is $E^2/4$ and the rms value is $E/2$. A sine-wave input will generate a square-wave error signal, and we must subtract out the fundamental since it just represents a slight change in gain, but not distortion. The rest of the error signal then represents distortion, and the rms total harmonic distortion (THD) for a sine wave is $0.217E$. We must relate this error to our allowable idle noise error. The following list gives the rms value of a full-scale-to-full-scale sine wave in terms of the bit size q for different numbers of bits in the converter:

n	rms
12	$1448q$
13	$2897q$
14	$5793q$
15	$11587q$
16	$23174q$

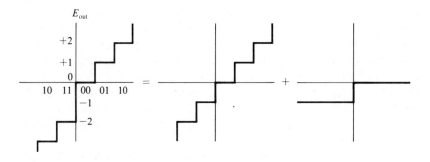

Fig. 2.5. D/A input/output characteristic with error due to inaccurate two's-complement carry around 0. A certain liberty has been taken in showing the abscissa as a continuous variable since the code is discrete.

We require our rms noise or THD to be 100 dB below the value just given for 16 bits. For the random input we have

$$E/2 \leq 23174 \, q \times 10^{-5}$$
$$E \leq 0.46 \, q.$$

For the sine wave input we have

$$0.217E \leq 23174 \, q \times 10^{-5}$$
$$E \leq 1.07 \, q.$$

It is not clear which input is closer to reality, and we would get the same answer for both if we didn't subtract out the signal component from the distortion for the sine wave input. I opt for the random input. In any case, the implication is that we must have a very good (expensive) 16-bit A/D converter. One can argue that we don't really work at the Nyquist bandwidth, but most systems do run from 70% to 80% of the Nyquist bandwidth, so you won't gain much there. The argument might continue that we don't really have to be 100 dB down because all the other idle noise sources did not live up to their allocation. True, but there's always something we forget, so a little conservatism will make up for it. However one squirms, it is difficult to avoid the conclusion that if a 16-bit system is going to be used, it cannot be a "sloppy" one, because it is precisely at the carries that sloppy converters make errors.

The converter we have just analyzed is a two's-complement converter. One can also use sign-magnitude (or absolute value) A/D and D/A converters. These are commonly realized by using an absolute-value amplifier in front of a unipolar A/D converter, and following a unipolar D/A converter. This type of converter has the advantage that the codes around 0 are determined by the lower-order bits so that the fractional accuracies on the bit weights are relaxed compared to the two's-complement converters for errors around 0. At higher levels of signal, the requirements on the two types of converters are similar, but at these levels it is the dynamic noise that is important and lower signal-to-noise ratios suffice.

There are also problems for the unwary in a sign-magnitude design. If the sign decision is not done properly, offsets in the absolute value amplifier can give rise to jumps or flats in the transfer characteristic similar to that in figure 2.5, and with the same results. There is another form of error in the D/A converter which can be avoided if the sample-and-hold or strobed amplifier follows the absolute-value amplifier in the output chain. Many absolute-value schemes involve two amplifiers and have different time delays for positive and negative signals. This sign-dependent time delay gives rise to a dynamic distortion which is proportional to the amplitude and frequency of the signal. By clocking the output change after this variable time delay, the distortion is avoided.

Range-Changing Systems

We defer discussion of dynamic noise sources and consider one alternative solution to achieving a wide dynamic range without undue expense. Once the input signal is more than 70 dB above the idle noise, the full resolution of a 16-bit converter is not required; instead, the requirement is that the signal-to-noise ratio be at least 70 dB. Figure 2.6 shows a system which changes gain (G) by factors of 2. It may be considered a floating-point system which always has a 12-bit mantissa and which changes gain whenever the signal goes through $1/16$, $1/8$, $1/4$, and $1/2$ of full scale. Although convenient, it is not necessary that the gains change by a factor of 2 or that a 12-bit converter be used. Lee and Lipschutz (1977) have reported on the requirements for different gain-changing ratios. The advantage of the system is that the LSB is now one part in 2^{12} of the total range instead of one part in 2^{16}, so the requirements on the carry at 0 are eased by a factor of 16.

Two types of ranging systems are in use. Lee and Lipschutz used an envelope ranging system in which signal increases cause upward ranging on a sample-to-sample basis to avoid clipping, but downward ranging is done on an envelope basis with a decay time of 50 to 100 ms. Kriz (1976) used a system in which the ranging is done instantaneously on a sample-to-sample basis. There are (at least) two problems with ranging systems. The signal-to-noise ratio jumps at range boundaries, and offsets and gain inaccuracies can cause discontinuities at the ranging points, which give rise to errors similar to those generated by the nonlinearity in figure 2.5. The envelope ranging system will be less sensitive to gain-change nonlinearities since range changes are made slowly, perhaps at a 20 to 30 Hz rate, and discontinuity noise will be confined to the lower frequencies. The instantaneous ranging system, on the other hand, has a higher signal-to-noise ratio if there is no discontinuity noise.

Figure 2.7 shows a plot of the S/N for 12-bit envelope and instantaneous ranging systems where *the only noise assumed is quantizing noise*. The curve is for a sine-wave input only; a random input would give a smoother curve. The 0 dB point on the ordinate corresponds to the maximum S/N ratio for the

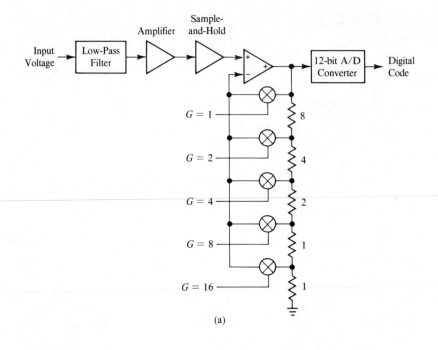

(a)

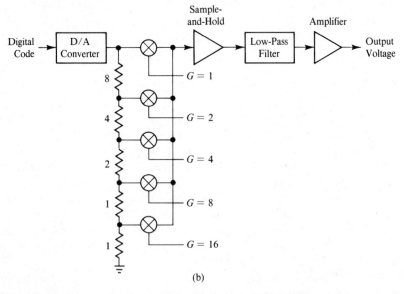

(b)

Fig. 2.6. Ranging A/D and D/A systems in power-of-2 steps

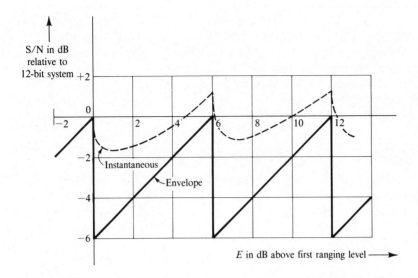

Fig. 2.7. S/N in 12-bit instantaneous and envelope ranging systems

converter, 74 dB for a 12-bit system in the Nyquist bandwidth. The abscissa is the ratio of the amplitude of the input to the voltage at the lowest gain-changing point.

With an envelope ranging system, once the signal exceeds the ranging point the converter will stay on that range and the quantizing noise (voltage) doubles. Therefore, the S/N drops by 6 dB at the ranging point and climbs again as the signal increases. With the instantaneous system, we have to calculate what fraction of the time the signal spent in each range in order to find the effective quantizing noise. Since this time is a function of the input waveshape, the curve is only good for a sine wave. For input levels greater than 12 dB above the first ranging point, the S/N curve comes very close to repeating the 6 to 12 dB portion of the curve every 6 dB. If one is making sine-wave tests, the envelope system is definitely worse than the instantaneous system. One can argue that in actual practice we should take some sort of average value over a range of inputs, in which case the instantaneous system would come out somewhat better, but then the envelope system would not show the sharp drop in S/N at the ranging points. If, in addition, we consider that the idle noise may be 8 dB above the quantizing noise on the lowest input range, the S/N just before the first range change will be 66 dB for a 12-bit system. Just after the gain change it will drop to 60 dB for the envelope system. As the signal increases, the idle noise becomes less significant and the dynamic noise and quantizing noise determine the S/N.

It is not clear on the basis of this discussion whether one should advocate more than 12 bits for a ranging system. In actual practice, 12 bits might be quite satisfactory; but if you have a specification based on sine-wave testing, you can be sure that somebody will test at the worst S/N point and reject the system. Twelve-bit converters are standard and relatively inexpensive. One is faced here with trading hard economics against what is probably very individual opinion. There are no simple answers.

DYNAMIC DISTORTION

In discussing dynamic noise or distortion, we will consider the simpler case of a nonranging converter, since in a ranging unit the quantizing noise will dominate at the higher input levels. If we wish to achieve a S/N of 70 dB and have 18 sources of noise, then for equal allocation of noise each source must be 82.6 dB below the signal.

It should be pointed out that for sine-wave testing, sampled systems are less tolerant of distortion than nonsampled systems. Third-harmonic distortion of a 15 kHz sine wave will produce a 45 kHz signal which will never be heard. In a system sampled at 50 kHz, however, the 45 kHz will beat with the sampling frequency to produce a very audible 5 kHz tone. It is not wise to belabor this point too much because the cubic characteristic that gives rise to the third harmonic will also produce third-order intermodulation distortion. The presence of 10 kHz and 15 kHz tones would then also give a 5 kHz beat tone ($2A - B$) in a continuous system. Sampled systems merely make the already controversial field of audio testing more difficult.

If the input and output filters are passive, they must be located in the system where the level is not too high, since we can expect the inductors to be nonlinear at large signal levels, and -82.6 dB is not much of a nonlinearity. The author has not been able to measure nonlinearities in a passive filter (less than -90 dB) at a 50 mV rms level, but has been informed that at a 1 V level, -75 dB distortion can be expected (Stockham 1976). Active filters will be subject to the same distortion sources as the amplifiers.

If standard IC operational amplifiers are used in an active filter (or as input preamplifiers), we can expect some moderate nonlinearity at full scale, crossover distortion about 0 from the class AB output stage, and slewing distortion with high-frequency, high-amplitude signals. The first two forms of distortion occur in the output section, so if the amplifiers have a reasonable gain-bandwidth (GBW) product, there will be enough loop gain at audio frequencies to reduce the output distortion to tolerable levels. The requirements are a little stiffer than one might at first think. A unity-gain noninverting amplifier with a GBW of 3 MHz will have a loop gain of 300 at 10 kHz. To keep the closed-loop distortion 82.6 dB below the signal, the open-loop output-stage distortion must be less than 2.2%. This, of course, is just an order-of-magnitude calculation, since the distortion products are at higher frequencies where the loop gain is less. If one is going to take some gain from the amplifier, then a higher GBW is required (and available). Unfortunately, different amplifier designs vary widely in their crossover distortion, and caution and a distortion analyzer are advised before designing them into a system.

Every amplifier has a slewing limit, which is defined as the maximum rate at which the output can change (Jung, Stephens, and Todd 1977). Some of the older designs have different limits for positive- and negative-going signals, but most of the newer designs are symmetrical. A sine wave of peak amplitude E and frequency f has a maximum rate of change around 0 of

$$\frac{de}{dt} = 2\pi Ef. \tag{2.5}$$

For a 10 V peak signal at 20 kHz, $de/dt = 1.26$ V/μs. If the amplifier cannot slew at this rate, it will tend to turn a sine wave into a triangular wave with resulting severe distortion. Jung, Stephens, and Todd (1977) have shown that for small distortions, the percent distortion (which is odd harmonic for a symmetrical amplifier) increases as the square of the output voltage and the cube of the frequency. Fortunately, the requirements on the amplifier for avoiding slewing distortion are not severe by today's standards. For a symmetrically slewing amplifier with a bipolar input stage, the dominant distortion is third-harmonic. The peak magnitude of the third harmonic *referred to the input terminals of the amplifier* is given by

$$E_{3p} = 2V_0 (0.0833 \, A^3) \tag{2.6}$$

where $V_0 = 26$ mV at 300° K and $A = $ (maximum rate of change of output)/ (amplifier slew limit). This formula is from the author's own analysis but will lead to the same answers as Jung, Stephens, and Todd (1977) for the same amplifier.

Assume a unity-gain noninverting amplifier with a peak output voltage of 10 V. For this case the peak input voltage is also 10 V. For the third harmonic to be 82.6 dB down from 10 V, it must be less than 741 μV. If we solve for A from equation 2.6, we find that $A \leq 0.555$, so the amplifier slew limit must be greater than $1.26/0.555 = 2.27$ V/μs. If we were taking a gain of 10 from the amplifier with the same peak output voltage, the third harmonic *referred to the input* would have to be less than 74.1 μV. Using equation 2.6 again, we arrive at a requirement of 4.89 V/μs for the amplifier. For an inverting connection using input and feedback resistors, E_{3p} should be divided by the attenuation from the input to the error point with the output grounded. So for most applications, a slewing rate of 5 V/μs is quite adequate. There are many amplifiers that meet this requirement, but one obviously must avoid 741s!

The sample-and-hold is subject to the same nonlinearities as the amplifier. In addition, sampling jitter manifests itself here. If the system clock jitters or if there is noise on the control lines, the actual sampling time will vary from pulse to pulse with respect to the assumed time. Figure 2.8 shows a sine wave with (highly exaggerated) timing jitter $\Delta T(t)$. We assume that the desampling in the D/A converter is done perfectly, or that jitter there is independent of the sampling jitter. Liu and Stanley (1965) give a complete but difficult treatment. At time t, we really measure $f(t + \Delta T(t))$. We expand this in a Taylor's series to get

$$f(t + \Delta T(t)) = f(t) + f'(t) \cdot \Delta T(t) + \cdots . \qquad (2.7)$$

In any practical system, terms in $(\Delta T(t))^2$ and beyond will be negligible. The second term in the expansion represents the error caused by sampling jitter. We assume that $f'(t)$ and $\Delta T(t)$ are independent with 0 mean. The mean square noise voltage caused by the sampling jitter is then

$$\overline{[f'(t) \cdot \Delta T(t)]^2} = \overline{[f'(t)]^2} \, \overline{[\Delta T(t)]^2} . \qquad (2.8)$$

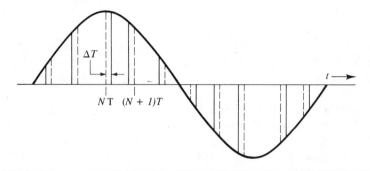

Fig. 2.8. Sine wave sampled with (exaggerated) timing jitter. $\Delta T(t)$ represents the deviation of the actual sampling time (solid lines) from the ideal sampling time (dotted lines).

The rms value of the error is just the square root of this expression. If we let $f(t)$ be a sine wave of frequency f and peak amplitude E, we have

$$\text{rms jitter error} = \frac{2\pi E f}{\sqrt{2}}(\Delta T_{rms})$$

$$= 2\pi E_{rms} f_s (\Delta T_{rms}). \qquad (2.9)$$

If the jitter error is to be 82.6 dB below the *rms* level of the signal, we have

$$\Delta T_{rms} \le \frac{1.18 \times 10^{-5}}{f}. \qquad (2.10)$$

If f is 10 kHz, the rms timing jitter must be less than 1.18 nsec. The result is real, measurable, and not to be ignored.

Feedthrough in the sample-and-hold during the conversion is a relatively minor problem in a well-designed unit. If the feedthrough is too large, the converter has a varying input during conversion which can lead to distortion. We can get a very rough idea of the numbers involved in the following way: A successive approximation converter with a mildly varying input will produce as an output some value which the input had between the start and the end of conversion (provable but not obvious). Because of this, we can assume that we are sampling the input with a peak-to-peak time jitter equal to the conversion time. We assume all times in the conversion interval equally likely, so that the rms time jitter is the conversion time divided by $\sqrt{12}$. We now use equation 2.9 with the rms jitter error equal to -82.6 dB down from the input to the sample-and-hold. For E_{rms} we use kE_{in}, where k is the amount of feedthrough attenuation we will solve for. For ΔT_{rms} we use the conversion time divided by $\sqrt{12}$. If we do this for a frequency of 10 kHz and a conversion time of 20 μs, we find that k must be less than -73.5 dB. Most decent sample-and-holds are on the order of 80 dB and better for feedthrough attenuation, so it is not a serious source of error.

Of course, both the A/D and the D/A can have nonuniform code widths at other places than 0. The analysis is similar to that given previously around 0 except the error rectangular wave no longer has a 50-50 duty cycle, and the duty cycle depends on the amplitude of the signal. If we assume we have a maximum sine wave and the error duty cycle is close to 50-50, then to meet the noise requirement,

$$0.217\, E \le \frac{23174q}{13490},$$

where 13490 corresponds to 82.6 dB. Then $E \leq 7.9q$, where E is the magnitude of the error, and q is 1 bit. The dynamic noise requirements impose much milder constraints on the linearity of the converters than the idle noise (low-level signals) requirements.

Output Circuitry Dynamic Errors

Although D/A converters are regarded as simpler devices than A/D converters, there are many ways that they can contribute errors to a high-fidelity system. We have already mentioned the problem of varying time delay in some absolute-value systems. In addition, there are glitches, slew-limiting in the output amplifier, and timing jitter in the DAC update pulses. The holding characteristic of the DAC also introduces a rolloff in the frequency response, which is, however, a compensatable linear effect.

A DAC glitch is an unwanted transient that occurs when the DAC changes state. If the peak value of the transient is small enough so that amplifiers following the DAC are not driven into a nonlinear state, then we are only interested in the area under the glitch, since the output filter's weighting function tends to average short-duration signals. If the area under the transient is proportional to the signal (which never happens), or is a constant independent of the signal, as in strobed amplifiers or sample-and-hold deglitchers, no output distortion will be introduced by the glitch. In an ordinary DAC the transient area is essentially independent of the signal, although it varies with the code change in the DAC, thereby producing distortion.

Glitches have two primary causes. First, bits cannot be switched on and off simultaneously. Therefore, whenever two or more bits must change at the same time, a transient excess or deficit of current occurs in the DAC network, partly because of digital time delays and partly because of signal propagation delays in the resistor summing network. Second, there is inevitable capacitive coupling from the digital switching signals through the switches, as well as stray coupling (a situation not helped by cramming many circuits together in small packages).

In a typical two's-complement DAC (fig. 2.4), the "sign" or 2^0 switch is turned on when its input is a logic 0, while all other bits are turned on when their inputs are 1's. Since the worst glitches occur when the maximum number of bits are changing, the worst transient is found when the digital input changes sign—that is, when it changes from 100. . .0 to 011. . .1 or the reverse.

If the 2^0 bit switches off 10 ns before all the other bits switch on, the fixed offset current that represents full scale is on for 10 ns. In a typical moderate-speed DAC, this current is about 2 mA, so that the transient charge introduced into the amplifier summing junction is 2 mA $\times$ 10 ns = 20 pC. In addition, each switch requires about a 2 V swing and has a coupling capacitance of 2 pF. Therefore, since $C = Q/V$, each switch can introduce 4 pC into the summing junction. There is usually a resistor between the first four switches and the rest of the DAC network. Its primary function is to attenuate current from those switches that correspond to the less significant bits so that individual current-determining resistors need not be so large. It also assures that only the first 4 bits have a major influence on the glitch area. Since the sign-bit capacitive coupling is in the opposite direction to the other three switches, the net capacitive coupling is 8 pC.

For the timing unbalance chosen, the capacitive coupling is in the opposite direction to the current unbalance so that the net coupling is 12 pC. The timing unbalance could just as easily have occurred in the other direction, giving a net charge of 28 pC. We will use an average value of 20 pC. We assume, as a first approximation, that when the code changes sign in the opposite direction, the coupling has the same magnitude but opposite sign. Smaller glitches occur at the 1/2 full-scale transition, still smaller ones at the 1/4 and 3/4 transitions, and so on.

If a small sampled sine wave with no dc offset is put through the DAC, there will be a glitch at each 0 crossing (fig. 2.9). A Fourier analysis of this series of pulses contains the fundamental and odd harmonics. Furthermore, because of the impulse approximation (we consider only the area under the glitch, not its shape), all odd harmonics have the same value of current, $4Qf$, where f is the frequency of the sine wave and Q is the impulse charge. If Q is 20 pC and f is 10 kHz, the peak harmonic current is 0.8 μA, 68 dB down from a full-scale sine wave. To be 82.6 dB down, Q would have to be 3.7 pC; and to be 100 dB down (one can make a case for considering glitches as idle noise for a two's-complement DAC), Q has to be less than 0.5 pC. These very severe requirements on the glitch area are the reason that most high-fidelity designs use deglitchers or output strobing. For voltage output DACs, the glitch area is given by manufacturers in volt-seconds. For a 10 V full-scale DAC, the area would have to be less than 19 V-ns to correspond to the 82.6 dB spec at 10 kHz, and less than 2.5 V-ns at the 100 dB spec.

Timing Jitter

If the timing pulses that define the final output transitions of the DAC have jitter on them, noise will be produced in the output. The expression for the noise depends on whether the output is held from one sample to the next (fig. 2.10), or whether the output is grounded for a short time between samples (a strobed output as in fig. 2.11).

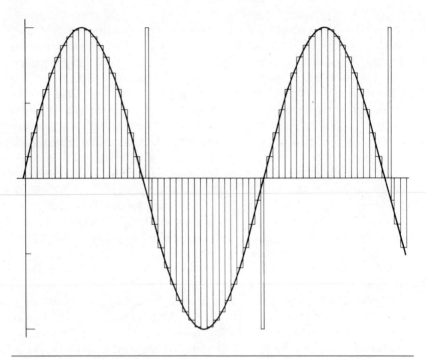

Fig. 2.9. Glitches resulting from a major carry in a DAC

Consider first the case where the output is held between samples. If an analog cosine wave $e(t) = A \cos(\omega t)$ is converted to digital form by sampling every T seconds, the change between two successive samples at the DAC output can be written as

$$\Delta e(nT) = e(nT) - e[(n - 1)T], \quad \text{where } n \text{ is an indexing variable} \quad (2.11)$$

$$= A \cos(\omega nT) - A \cos[\omega(n - 1)T] \quad (2.12)$$

$$= 2A \sin\left(\frac{\omega T}{2}\right) \sin(\omega nT + \theta), \quad \theta = \tan^{-1}\left[\frac{1 - \cos(\omega T)}{-\sin(\omega T)}\right] \quad (2.13)$$

where all angles are to be taken in radians. The difference between successive samples is a sine wave with amplitude and phase which is a function of frequency. Figure 2.10 shows that the noise pulse caused by the time jitter has an amplitude $\Delta e(nT)$ as given by equation 2.13, a polarity depending on whether the jittered pulse is leading or lagging its correct position, and a pulse width

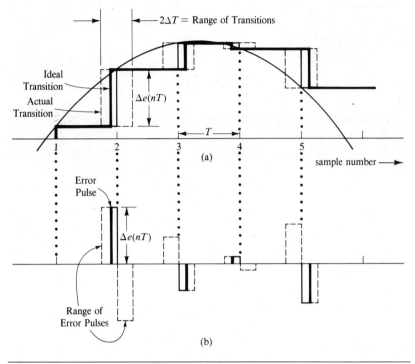

Fig. 2.10. D/A timing jitter in a held system. The polarity of the error signal (b) depends on whether the jittered pulse is leading or lagging its correct position.

equal to the magnitude of the jitter error. We may regard successive samples of noise-pulse width as samples from a random variable with a probability density distribution given by the jitter. The area under the noise pulse is given by the product of $\Delta e(nT)$ and the pulse width. The rms noise is given by the rms area averaged over one period, T. Since we assume that the amplitude and the time jitter are statistically independent with 0 mean, the rms area is just the product

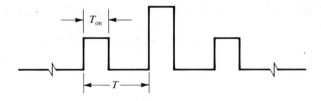

Fig. 2.11. D/A timing jitter in a strobed system

of the rms value of $\Delta e(nT)$ and the rms value $\Delta \tau$ of the jitter. We therefore have for the rms noise voltage

$$e_{rms} = \frac{\Delta \tau}{T} \sqrt{2} \, A \, \sin\left(\frac{\omega T}{2}\right). \qquad (2.14)$$

As mentioned previously, Bennett (1956) has shown that sampling wideband noise is equivalent to sampling noise of the same rms value, but band-limited to the Nyquist frequency. If the output filter has a noise equivalent bandwidth F_B (essentially its 3 dB point), the output rms noise is given by

$$e_{OH} = e_{rms} \sqrt{\frac{F_B}{F_{Ny}}}$$

$$= \frac{\Delta \tau}{T} \sqrt{2} \, A \, \sin\left(\frac{\omega T}{2}\right) \sqrt{\frac{F_B}{F_{Ny}}}. \qquad (2.15)$$

The sampling frequency $F_S = 1/T$, and $F_{Ny} = F_S/2$; if we use $\omega = 2\pi f$, we may write equation 2.15 as

$$e_{OH} = 2A \, \sin\left(\frac{\pi f}{F_S}\right) \Delta \tau F_S \sqrt{\frac{F_B}{F_S}}. \qquad (2.16)$$

Equation (2.16) is the rms noise out of the output filter caused by time jitter in a full-period hold system. The signal-to-noise ratio is given by

$$\left(\frac{S}{N}\right)_{JITTER_H} = \frac{1}{\sqrt{8} \, \sin\left(\frac{\pi f}{F_S}\right) \Delta \tau F_S \sqrt{\frac{F_B}{F_S}}}. \qquad (2.17)$$

For a strobed output system (fig. 2.11) the amplitude of the error pulse is given by $A \cos(\omega nT)$ since the output pulse always starts from ground. We also assume that the leading and trailing edges of the strobe pulse are jittered independently (a very reasonable assumption for practical systems). The noise from the output filter is derived in much the same way and is given by

$$e_{OS} = \sqrt{2} \, A \Delta \tau F_S \sqrt{\frac{F_B}{F_S}}, \qquad (2.18)$$

and we assume that the leading and trailing edge jitter has the same rms value $\Delta\tau$. For an on-time T_{ON}, the output signal is $(T_{ON}/T)A\cos(\omega nT)$, and the signal-to-noise ratio for the strobed case is given by

$$\left(\frac{S}{N}\right)_{JITTER_S} = \frac{T_{ON}/T}{2\Delta\tau F_S\sqrt{\dfrac{F_B}{F_S}}}. \qquad (2.19)$$

Using equation 2.17 we calculate the rms jitter allowed in the held case for an 82.6 dB S/N ratio for a 50 kHz sampling frequency, a 20 kHz output filter bandwidth, and a signal frequency of 10 kHz. The rms jitter must be less than 1.4 ns, a reasonable number to meet in practice, but probably requiring a crystal oscillator for timing, as well as transition times in the logic more compatible with TTL than with CMOS.

For the strobed case we assume that the parameters are the same, and the output is grounded for 5 μs out of the 20 μs period. We find that for an 82.6 dB S/N ratio the rms jitter must be less than 0.88 ns, independent of the signal frequency.

One should not draw any conclusions from the above derivation about the virtues of a held system over a strobed system; the prime purpose is to set bounds on how good the timing system has to be.

Output Slew Limiting

Slew-limiting problems arise in the output amplifier as well as in the input. Because the DAC output is pulsed rather than continuous, the problems are less obvious, and first-order thinking can lead to trouble. The DAC output can be held or strobed, and we can have three cases of slew limiting: full limiting for the whole transition, going in and out of limiting, and just coming close to limiting as in the analysis for the continuous case of the input amplifier. In the interest of brevity, we shall treat the case of full limiting for the held and strobed output. We shall also assume symmetrical limiting for positive and negative signals. Amplifiers that limit asymmetrically are not suitable for DAC outputs anyhow because they are too slow, and the analysis does not add any insight. Besides, the only major difference is that both even and odd harmonics are present, whereas symmetrical limiting produces only odd harmonics.

For full symmetric slew limiting (fig. 2.12) we assume the output always makes a transition from one level to the next at its maximum rate de/dt. For the case of the held output, the derivative signal in figure 2.12c makes most clear

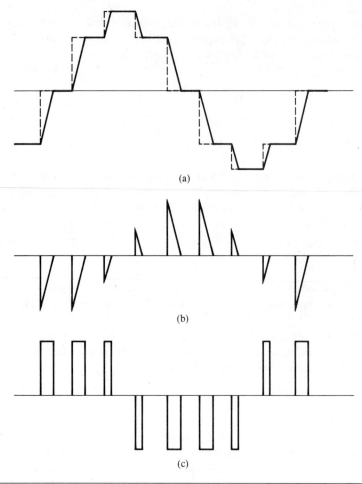

(a)

(b)

(c)

Fig. 2.12.   Symmetric slew limiting for a held DAC. (a) Output signal; (b) The difference between the actual output and the ideal 0 transition time output (the error signal); (c) The derivative of the output signal.

the nature of the slew-limited waveform; it has a constant amplitude (de/dt) and a variable width, thereby giving it the characteristics of a pulse-duration modulated signal.

The error signal can be expanded in a double Fourier series by a method developed by Bennett (Schwartz, Bennett, and Stein 1966). The coefficients in this series give the amplitudes of the distortion products and of all the beat frequencies of the distortion products as well as the amplitudes of the sampling frequency and its harmonics. Having gone through this jungle of infinite Bessel-function series, the author can state with confidence that the following approximate analysis gives very accurate results for any practical case.

The amplitude of the error signal in figure 2.12b is the difference between any two successive DAC outputs. This was given in equation 2.13 as

$$\Delta e(nT) = 2A \sin\left(\frac{\omega T}{2}\right) \sin(\omega nT + \theta). \tag{2.13}$$

We shall use the impulse approximation again, that is, we approximate the error waveform by an impulse at the ideal transition time with an area equal to the area of the error waveform. The error signal has an amplitude of $\Delta e(nT)$ and a base duration of $\Delta e(nT)/(de/dt)$. Its area is therefore

$$\frac{1}{2} \frac{\Delta e(nT)^2}{de/dt}. \tag{2.20}$$

We note immediately the source of slew-limiting distortion; the error signal is proportional to the *square* of the difference between successive DAC outputs. Since the error-signal polarity follows $\Delta e(nT)$, the complete description for its area is

$$-\frac{1}{2} \frac{\Delta e(nT)^2}{de/dt} \, \text{sgn}[\Delta e(nT)], \tag{2.21}$$

where $\text{sgn}(x)$ is equal to $+1$ whenever x is positive, and -1 whenever x is negative. The minus sign in front of equation 2.21 arises because we defined the error to be actual-ideal. We shall ignore it in the sequel.

If we substitute equation 2.13 into equation 2.21 we will have an expression for the area under the error waveform. This area averaged over one sampling period T gives the magnitude of the error signal that modulates the sampling pulse train and gives sidebands around dc, the sampling frequency, and all its harmonics. We have

$$\text{Error} = \frac{2A^2 \sin^2\left(\dfrac{\omega T}{2}\right)}{T \dfrac{de}{dt}} \sin^2(\omega nT + \theta) \, \text{sgn}[\sin(\omega nT + \theta)] \tag{2.22}$$

If we change the time variable from nT to t, we can make a straightforward Fourier analysis of the error signal. This time switch may seem a little confusing, but what we have derived is the continuous signal which, if sampled, would give the same area to the sampling impulse as is under the error waveform in figure 2.12b. The error signal contains odd harmonics only; the amplitude of the kth harmonic is given by

$$
b_k = \frac{16A^2 \sin^2 \left(\dfrac{\omega T}{2}\right)}{\pi k(k^2 - 4)T \dfrac{de}{dt}}, \qquad k = 1, 3, 5, 7 \ldots . \tag{2.23}
$$

Note that these distortion terms ($k = 1$ represents a gain change) also modulate with the sampling frequency and its harmonics. A 15 kHz signal would give rise to an inaudible 45 kHz third harmonic; but in a system sampled at 50 kHz there would be a beat note at 5 kHz. To a very good approximation, the amplitude of the beat is given by the amplitude of the harmonic causing the beat. The harmonic magnitudes given by equation 2.23 are peak values; therefore, the rms-signal-to-rms-harmonic ratio is given by

$$
\left(\frac{S}{N}\right)_k = \frac{\pi k(k^2 - 4)T \dfrac{de}{dt}}{16A \sin^2 \left(\dfrac{\omega T}{2}\right)} \quad \text{(held output).} \tag{2.24}
$$

We shall leave equation 2.24 as it is, although it can be massaged in various ways. $T(de/dt)$ is the maximum amount the output can change in one sampling period, A is the peak amplitude of the output, and $\omega T/2$ is $\pi f/F_S$.

Let us calculate what de/dt has to be to keep the ratio of signal to third-harmonic beat 82.6 dB down for a sampling frequency of 50 kHz, a signal frequency of 15 kHz (giving a 5 kHz beat), and a peak output A of 10 V. The slewing rate de/dt must be greater than 4.7 V/ns! The result seems absurd, but what it says is that the output must not be allowed to slew limit (Kriz 1975). The small-signal response of the output amplifier must be controlled, most conveniently by a capacitor around the feedback resistor, so that the output rate as calculated from the linear response never exceeds the slewing rate. One can make a calculation for the distortion under these conditions, but the result is quite close to the continuous case; if the slewing rate is at least two to four times the maximum output rate, the distortion will be acceptably low.

Slewing Distortion with a Strobed Output

We include this case, illustrated in figure 2.13, because it has given rise to some misconceptions. The argument goes that if the slewing rate is symmetrical, we

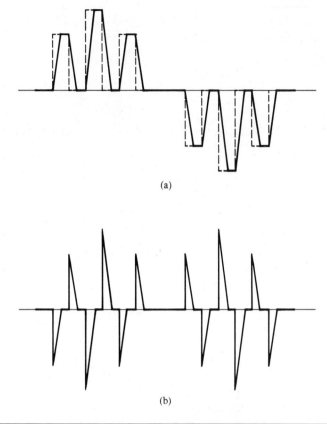

(a)

(b)

Fig. 2.13. Symmetric slew limiting for a strobed DAC. (a) Output signal; (b) The difference between the actual output and the ideal 0 transition time output (the error signal); see figure 2.12.

gain as much area on the trailing edge as we lose on the leading edge, and therefore there is no loss of signal area due to slewing, which thereby results in no distortion. The argument is almost correct; however, the compensating area occurs at a later time! The Fourier series for the trailing-edge error waveform has the opposite sign from the leading-edge error, and the typical harmonic has the form $\sin[k\omega(t - T_{\text{ON}})]$ as opposed to $\sin(k\omega t)$ for the leading-edge error waveform.

Because the output always starts from 0, the amplitude of the error waveform $\Delta e(nT)$ is just $A \cos(\omega T)$ rather than the more complicated form of equation

2.13 for the held case. As a result, the amplitude of the kth harmonic for the leading-edge waveform is given by

$$c_k = \frac{4A^2}{\pi k(k^2 - 4)T\dfrac{de}{dt}}. \tag{2.25}$$

The kth harmonic voltage for the total error waveform (leading- and trailing-edge errors) is given by

$$e_k = c_k \cos(k\omega t) - c_k \cos[k\omega(t - T_{ON})] \tag{2.26}$$

$$= 2c_k \sin\left(\frac{k\omega T_{ON}}{2}\right) \sin\left[k\omega\left(t - \frac{T_{ON}}{2}\right)\right]. \tag{2.27}$$

The amplitude c'_k of the kth harmonic when both leading and trailing edges are summed is therefore

$$c'_k = \frac{8A^2 \sin\left(\dfrac{k\omega T_{ON}}{2}\right)}{\pi k(k^2 - 4)T\dfrac{de}{dt}}. \tag{2.28}$$

(There is an implicit assumption here that the slewing rate is fast enough so the output always reaches 0 between pulses.) Equation 2.28 should be compared to equation 2.23. The harmonic amplitude is also a function of frequency for the strobed case since the cancellation of leading and trailing edges is more complete at lower frequencies. Any asymmetry between the leading and trailing edges will increase the harmonic magnitude. Note also that in the limit, $T_{ON} = T$, equation 2.28 does not go over to equation 2.23. We are dealing with non-linear effects and superposition does not hold!

The rms-signal-to-rms-harmonic ratio is given by

$$\left(\frac{S}{N}\right)_k = \frac{\pi k(k^2 - 4)T\dfrac{de}{dt}\dfrac{T_{ON}}{T}}{8A \sin\left(\dfrac{k\omega T_{ON}}{2}\right)} \quad \text{(strobed output).} \tag{2.29}$$

The term T_{ON}/T is introduced because the duty cycle makes the signal amplitude $(T_{ON}/T)A$. We calculate what de/dt must be to keep the ratio of signal to third-harmonic beat at -82.6 dB for a sampling frequency of 50 kHz, a signal frequency of 15 kHz, a peak output A of 10 V, and an on-time T_{ON} of 15 μs. The slewing rate must be greater than 1.3 V/ns. Although this number is less than we calculated for the held case (4.7 V/ns), it is impressively large, and points out that the area cancellation argument does not hold much water.

As pointed out in the section on timing jitter, these derivations do not really show up the superiority of one method of output deglitching over the other. Here they both make abundantly clear that the output must not slew limit.

CONCLUSIONS, COMMENTS, AND CAVEATS

There are additional topics that could be discussed, such as the complexity of the input and output filters for preventing aliasing (input) and avoiding possible overload of following analog equipment. Filter designs would take us too far afield from the hardware limitations with which this discussion is concerned. One comment should be made, however. Slot (1971) has pointed out that in *continuous* systems, too sharp a cutoff filter (more than 6 dB/octave) makes the music sound more shrill, and the author has heard comments about "ringing" in digital audio systems. Since a sharp-cutoff filter is required to keep a reasonable sampling rate while holding the aliasing noise to acceptable limits, some additional perceptual research is called for in this area.

The filter problem points up one of the major difficulties in trying to set specifications for audio systems. There is not really a good test signal, such that if the equipment meets all specifications with that signal, it will sound superb with music, even to "golden ears." This discussion has used a mixture of random inputs and sine waves to set specifications. Limits have been set in terms of rms noise and distortion, but the ear is not an rms device. Small infrequent clicks may have a very low rms value, but they sound very objectionable; perhaps if their rms value were calculated over the ear's integration time, the calculated and perceptual responses might be closer. The rms specification enables us to set limits on each type of distortion under the assumption that their effects add independently, as noise power does. The ear may not agree with this approach. We must also point out that some of the specifications seem very severe. Any *one* source of noise or distortion at these levels would never be heard. It is only because we assume that they are all present simultaneously and add as noise power that each effect must be so small. One doesn't have to go with these numbers, but the results should allow the system designer to see how the noise and distortion change as various design parameters are traded off.

Lastly, many of the perceptual tests on which the limits are based are done under very controlled laboratory conditions which are not duplicated in one's living room. The author listens to classical music in the morning on a small FM radio in the kitchen with a children's TV program going on in the next room. Listening conditions are not ideal, but the music is still enjoyable. We should not let ourselves get into the state where, to quote from Flanders and Swann's song *High Fidelity,* ". . . we never cared for music much, it's the high fidelity!"

REFERENCES

Bennett, W. R. 1948. Spectra of quantized signals. *Bell System Technical Journal* 27(4):16–72.

Bennett, W. R. 1956. Methods of solving noise problems. *Proceedings of the IRE* 44:609–38.

Blesser, B. 1978. Digitization of audio. *Journal of the Audio Engineering Society* 26(10):739–71.

Blesser, B., B. Locanthi, and T. Stockham, eds. 1983. *Digital audio.* New York: Audio Engineering Society.

Jung, W. G., M. L. Stephens, and C. C. Todd. 1977. Slewing induced distortion and its effects on audio amplifier performance—with correlated measurement/listening results. 57th AES Convention, Los Angeles, AES Preprint 1252(G-7).

Kozinn, Allan. 1980. The future is digital. *N. Y. Times* April 13. Sunday Magazine Section, Part 2, pp. 84–93.

Kriz, J. 1975. A 16-bit ADA conversion system for high fidelity audio research. *IEEE Transactions on Audio and Electroacoustics* AU–23:146–49.

Kriz, J. 1976. Audio analog-digital-analog conversion system. 55th AES Convention, New York, AES Preprint 1142(L-2).

Lee, F. F., and D. Lipschutz. 1977. Floating point encoding for transcription of high fidelity audio signals. *Journal of the Audio Engineering Society* 25(5):266–72.

Liu, B., and T. P. Stanley. 1965. Error bounds for jittered sampling. *IEEE Transactions on Automatic Control* AC–10:449–54.

Nakajima, Heitaro, Toshitada Doi, Jyoji Fukuda, and Akira Iga. 1983. *Dijitaru odio gijutsu nyūmon.* Translated as *Digital audio technology.* Blue Ridge Summit, Pa.: Tab Books.

Olson, H. F. 1947. *Elements of acoustical engineering.* New York: Van Nostrand.

Schwartz, M., W. R. Bennett, and S. Stein. 1966. *Communications systems and techniques.* New York: McGraw-Hill.

Slot, G. 1971. *Audio quality.* New York: Drake Publications.

Stockham, T. G., Jr. 1971. A/D and D/A converters: Their effect on digital audio fidelity. 41st AES Convention, AES Preprint 834(D-1).

Stockham, T. G., Jr. 1976. Personal communication.

Talambiras, R. 1976. Digital-to-analog converters: Some problems in producing high fidelity signals. *Computer Design* 15:63–69.

Talambiras, R. 1977. Some considerations in the design of wide-dynamic-range audio digitizing systems. 57th AES Convention, Los Angeles, AES Preprint 1226(A-1).

Warnock, R. B. 1976. Longitudinal digital recording of audio. 55th AES Convention, New York, AES Preprint 1169(L-3).

3

ARCHITECTURAL ISSUES IN THE DESIGN OF THE SYSTEMS CONCEPTS DIGITAL SYNTHESIZER

Peter R. Samson

This is a discussion of the Systems Concepts digital synthesizer and of the reasoning behind various aspects of its architecture. In such a machine there are a great many design tradeoffs to be considered; this chapter describes how these issues were resolved for the biggest and most powerful digital music synthesizer of its time.

The fundamentals of the architecture are first summarized. Then, details of the device are discussed, categorized according to specific capabilities of the synthesizer rather than to specific components of the hardware. (Frequently, however, a design feature that is included to implement one capability can be used to facilitate a number of other capabilities.) These discussions include reasons for the particular detailed design decisions that were made. The actual hardware implementation, at the level of circuits and devices, is referred to only when it concerns the architectural decisions. Finally, the overall architectural characteristics of the synthesizer are reviewed in light of the foregoing details, and the underlying reasons are given for the top-level design. Note that throughout this article, the unit under discussion is the production-model synthesizer; this has a few modest enhancements when compared to the prototype unit, which is described elsewhere (Samson 1980).

DESIGN STARTING POINT

There are three common starting points for the design of a machine like this: (1) a performance specification; (2) a budget; (3) a particular architecture or hardware-implementation idea. While each of these aspects will in practice contribute significantly to the final architecture, typically *one* of them is the motivational source of the design, and will take precedence in the majority of conflicts. Some purely hypothetical illustrations of these starting points are given below.

1. A Performance Specification. "Let's make a synthesizer that can do Beethoven's *Ninth Symphony* in real time." If pressed, the author of this specification might be willing to cut it back to "just the last movement."
2. A Budget. The budget may be monetary, as in "Let's make the best synthesizer we can for *X* dollars;" or it may be technical, as in "Let's make the most powerful synthesizer we can that fits on this printed-circuit card." An aggressive designer might interpret the latter to permit parts hanging over the edge of the card.
3. An Architectural Idea. "Let's make a synthesizer with a source-data bus and a destination-data bus, and a lot of independent processing elements hung between them." Novelty, of course, is not necessary; it may even be suspect.

In the case of the Systems Concepts synthesizer, performance specifications were the ruling requirement. The intention was to provide a tool for serious work by composers and researchers into musical acoustics. To this end the synthesizer had to provide specific support for all the popular synthesis techniques, and at the same time have the flexibility necessary to permit experimentation in the development of new techniques.

There were no digital synthesizers in existence whose designs could be drawn on when this machine was being designed, so its performance specifications had to be determined at least partly by analogy with other means of synthesis. Four of these were considered: acoustic (i.e., mechanical) synthesis, as by conventional instruments; electronic analog synthesis; digital music synthesis on general-purpose computers; and digital speech synthesis. Before a firm specification was prepared, literature was surveyed in each of these areas. Furthermore, in the case of computer music—the most directly applicable of the four areas, as well as the most rapidly developing—discussions were held with prominent workers in the field to identify promising new developments.

As a rough guide to the magnitudes involved, it was decided that the machine was to have a real-time synthesis capability comparable to that of a string quartet, both by additive and by subtractive methods. (The numerical interpretation of this requirement was made quite conservatively and is discussed below.) A larger synthesizer (say, chamber-orchestra-sized), though obviously desirable, was judged infeasible with the technology available at the time the design was being done (1973–74). A smaller one (comparable, say, to a violin) would be far simpler to build; but it was concluded that someone trying to prepare a significant musical work on that synthesizer would continually be hemmed in and frustrated by its constraints.

SUMMARY DESCRIPTION

The machine that resulted from the performance requirements is very large and very fast. It is meant to be attached to a computer system in which it will perform high-speed synthesis and processing of digital signals. The control of this synthesizer is the responsibility of the host computer, which may derive its control information from statements the user prepares in some language or from real-time input devices for live performance. Among the synthesizer's distinctive characteristics are the following:

- Size—2500 integrated circuits
- Speed—20 million multiplications per second
- Word length—20 bits for signals; 12 to 30 bits for other quantities
- Configurability—a 256-location "patch panel" called *sum memory*
- Modes—each processing element having numerous alternative functions
- Sample rate—continuously variable (but see the section on timing, below)
- Delay memory—65 536 locations for delay lines and table lookup
- Analog I/O—up to 16 channels

- Digital I/O—multiple per-sample data streams in and out
- Maintenance aids—10% of hardware strictly for diagnostics

The variable sample rate deserves special comment because it affects nearly every architectural decision. Since computation takes time, there is a tradeoff: more complexity of computation versus a higher sampling rate. This synthesizer permits the choice of sampling rate to be made by the user, rather than by the hardware designer, in accordance with the musical requirements of each particular application. In other words, the architecture must accomodate a range of sample rates rather than being optimized for one specific rate. A survey of computer-music practice indicated that a reasonable range would be from 18 kHz to 50 kHz, with the geometric mean of 30 kHz as a typical value.

Basic Structure

The three types of computational elements in the synthesizer are generators, modifiers, and delay units. These names describe the most common uses of the elements, but should not be taken restrictively: generators can modify signals, modifiers can generate them, delay units can do waveshaping, and so on. For each type of computational element there is a specific collection of hardware. All of the generators have their work done by the generator calculator; all of the modifiers, by the modifier calculator; and all of the delay units, by the delay unit calculator. Sometimes it is convenient to speak of "the generator," meaning the hardware that applies to all generators; and likewise for the other elements.

Time Multiplexing

Each of the calculators is time-multiplexed: the generator calculator, for instance, first does the work for generator 0; then for generator 1; and so on for as many generators as have been designated in use. At the same time that the generator calculator starts on generator 0, the modifier calculator starts on modifier 0, and the delay unit calculator starts on delay unit 0. The three calculators run simultaneously. Each active generator, modifier, and delay unit must have its work done exactly once in each sample period. In this architecture, the identity of a given processing element is equivalent to an address in a control memory. Generator 5, for instance, is simply the data at location 5 in the generator control memory. This data can be said to comprise the parameters of the given processing element. Some of these parameters—the choice of waveshape, for instance—are changed only upon command from the host computer. Others—the phase angle of an oscillator, for example—will be modified in each sample period.

Generators

Control memory space is provided in the generator calculator for 256 generators. Each generator has all of the following basic capabilities:

- Oscillation—sine, sawtooth, square, pulse train, or buzz waveforms (the last type of waveform is defined later under "Excitation Waveforms")
- Frequency modulation (FM)—input from sum memory
- Frequency sweep—built into generator (in addition to FM capability)
- Envelope generation—linear or exponential, rising or falling
- Amplitude control—oscillatory waveform multiplied by envelope

There are also a number of special generator modes, including those in which the generator passes data between sum memory and the host computer, the DACs, or the ADCs.

Modifiers

The modifier calculator provides for 128 modifiers. Based on its mode, which is set by command independently for each modifier, a modifier can do any of the following:

- Modulation—amplitude modulation or balanced modulation
- Mixing—combination of two inputs, each with its own gain coefficient
- Resonance—one or two poles
- Antiresonance—one or two zeros
- Noise generation—uniformly distributed (*white*) noise
- Nonlinear operations—clipping, rectification, zero-crossing detection
- Conditional operations—maximum, minimum, threshold, track-and-hold
- Reverberation (in conjunction with a delay unit)—all-pass reverb

Delay Units

The delay unit calculator has control memory for 32 delay units. The delay units are the means of access to delay memory, which comprises 65 536 locations. Each active delay unit has parameters that designate an area in the delay memory. Partitioning of the delay memory among delay units is done entirely by commands from the host computer; several delay units may refer to the same locations in delay memory. Depending on the mode of a delay unit, it uses its area of delay memory either as a delay line or as a stored table for lookup purposes. (The host computer can also read and write delay memory, though at a comparatively slow speed.) Each delay unit communicates data with the rest of the synthesizer through a modifier; the association between modifiers and delay units is completely flexible and is specified by parameters of the modifiers.

Timing

The basic unit of time within the synthesizer is called a *tick*: its duration is 195 ns. Each generator in use occupies the generator calculator for one tick; each modifier in use occupies the modifier calculator for two ticks; and each delay unit in use occupies the delay unit calculator for four ticks. Since the three calculators run at the same time, the total time required for computation in one sample period is whichever is greater: the number of generators in use, twice the number of modifiers in use, or four times the number of delay units in use. This result is the number of *processing ticks*.

The hardware design relies heavily on pipelining. This technique makes possible the high processing rates of the synthesizer, but it requires a certain number of *overhead ticks* which are spent filling the pipeline at the beginning of each sample period. The pipelines in this machine are eight stages long, and consequently the number of overhead ticks in each sample period is eight.

The user specifies the sample period to the synthesizer as an integral number of ticks, which must exceed the total number of processing ticks and update ticks. (The resolution unit, one tick, corresponds to about 1% resolution at 50 kHz, and proportionately finer resolution at lower sample rates.) The ticks in a sample period which are not overhead ticks, and which the user has not designated as processing ticks, are called *update ticks*. They are available for performance of commands from the host computer, one command per update tick. If no commands are pending, the synthesizer simply idles during the update tick. Figure 3.1 illustrates the sequence of ticks that comprise a sample period.

Sum Memory

Generators and modifiers pass data to one another through locations in sum memory. This is divided functionally into four *quadrants,* called SA, SB, SC, and SD, each with 64 locations. Quadrants SA and SB contain sums being formed during a given sample period; quadrants SC and SD have the final sums that were formed during the previous sample period. At the start of each sample period, the contents of the 64 locations of SA are copied into the corresponding locations of SC, and similarly from SB to SD; then all locations in SA and SB are set to 0. During the sample period, as each computational element is executed, it will read data from SC or SD (or both), calculate its result, and add that result into SA if it is a generator or into SB if it is a modifier. Parameters of

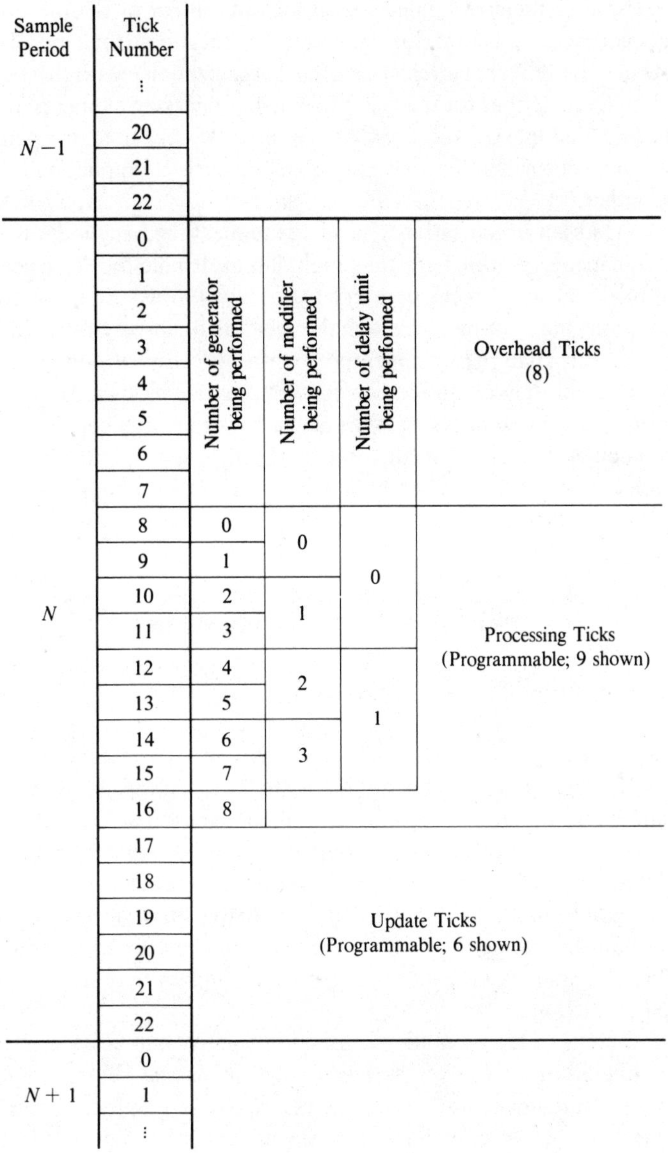

Sample Period	Tick Number	Number of generator being performed	Number of modifier being performed	Number of delay unit being performed	
	⋮				
N − 1	20				
	21				
	22				
N	0				Overhead Ticks (8)
	1				
	2				
	3				
	4				
	5				
	6				
	7				
	8	0	0	0	Processing Ticks (Programmable; 9 shown)
	9	1	0	0	
	10	2	1	0	
	11	3	1	0	
	12	4	2	1	
	13	5	2	1	
	14	6	3	1	
	15	7	3	1	
	16	8			
	17				Update Ticks (Programmable; 6 shown)
	18				
	19				
	20				
	21				
	22				
N + 1	0				
	1				
	⋮				

Fig. 3.1. Tick timing

each processing element designate which location in SA or SB the result is added into, and which location (for a generator) or locations (for a modifier) in SC and SD the required data is read from. This organization means that the user need have concern neither for the order in which processing elements are performed during a sample period, nor for the number of ticks (due to pipelining) that elapse between when a processing element reads its input and when it writes its output.

The four-quadrant organization also serves to meet the bandwidth requirements on sum memory, which are quite high: it must handle four read accesses and three read-add-write accesses every two ticks (390 ns). In the hardware implementation, the sum memory was the most difficult part of the design. This was not surprising. In a machine with a plurality of computational elements—whether they are implemented with separate hardware or by time-multiplexing—the interconnection of the elements is generally harder to design than the computational elements themselves. This is especially the case when the interconnections must be alterable upon command.

OVERALL DESIGN CONSIDERATIONS

Numeric Representation

One architectural decision, made quite early, was to use fixed-point rather than floating-point representation for numbers. To use floating-point (with the same requirements on processing speed) would have added at least 50% to the hardware cost; the basic advantage it would have offered is that the user would not have to pay attention to the scaling of quantities that occur during computation. The benefit is minor compared to the cost. So that this scaling can be done as needed, built-in scaling factors that can be set by the user are provided for the sine/buzz oscillator functions of the generator, and for each multiplication performed by each modifier.

Two's-complement representation is used for negative numbers. Most of the arithmetic operations in the synthesizer are additions and subtractions, and these are most straightforwardly implemented in two's-complement. Furthermore, it provides compatibility with the host computer, since nearly all current computers use two's-complement. Generally, signals are regarded as signed fractions, but there can be occasions when they are better interpreted as integers. To provide for these instances, the multiplications performed by a modifier can be either fractional or integer, depending on the modifier's mode.

Hard-wired versus Sequential Logic

One kind of design tradeoff came up repeatedly: that between hard-wired, dedicated hardware on the one hand, and sequential use of a more general-purpose structure on the other. The hard-wired approach runs faster; the sequential approach takes less equipment. As a rule of thumb, assuming a specific technology (and assuming the hardware has no spare capacity to begin with), to make something run n times faster requires n times as much hardware. Another form of this statement is as follows: to do n times the work, either multiply the hardware by n (e.g., duplicate it a total of n times), or time-multiplex the hardware n ways (taking n times as long). In this synthesizer, decisions of how much hardware to provide for a specific type of computation were rarely clear-cut. The choices were made mostly on the basis of the level of use the algorithms in question were receiving among computer musicians. If a number of people were getting worthwhile results by performing a certain calculation 50 times per sample, it was appropriate to try to provide that the synthesizer could accomplish that, too, at a satisfactory sample rate.

Powers of 2, Multiples of 4

There are two aspects of the hardware implementation whose consequences appear in almost every architectural specification. First, the number of words in a memory is generally a power of 2; second, the number of bits in a word is most often a multiple of 4. These are characteristics of the particular family of integrated circuits (TTL) used in the machine. This causes some numbers to be rounded up. If, for instance, a given calculation needs to be done to an accuracy of at least 15 bits, it costs almost nothing to go to 16.

ADDITIVE SYNTHESIS

The first set of algorithms to be considered in the design were those for additive synthesis. This technique forms a sound by adding up a number of components. Usually the components are sinusoidal. If their frequencies are related harmonically (and assuming constant amplitudes), the resulting sum waveform will be periodic. However, much of the capability of additive synthesis comes when the component frequencies and amplitudes are varied individually during the course of a note. Variations of this sort, though often small in magnitude, give much of the character and interest to notes played on acoustic instruments (Grey 1975; Moorer 1977). Since the component frequencies are not harmonically related, the resulting waveform is not periodic. For this reason, and because the individual components have envelopes of different shapes, sounds of comparable quality cannot be generated by playing a stored waveform, however complicated it may be; nor can it be done by crossfading between two such waveforms. For generality, this synthesizer does provide for stored waveforms, as described later. Where the choice exists, the architecture does not force the use of additive techniques (though one might say it is *partial* to them). A typical additive-synthesis configuration is shown in figure 3.2.

The Function of the Generator

The basic natural oscillation is an exponentially decaying sinusoid. This holds (in principle) for both mechanical and electrical oscillators, so the analogy was judged sufficiently strong to require a corresponding capability in every generator. There is no requirement that the digital synthesis process mimic the exact method of physical oscillation (for example, approximating the differential equations by difference equations). The only requirement is that it come up with equivalent results.

In this synthesizer, the sinusoid is computed in one part of the generator, and the exponential in another part; the two results are multiplied to produce the output of the generator. This organization gives the user separate control of frequency and amplitude, which are generally perceived as distinct aspects of a sound.

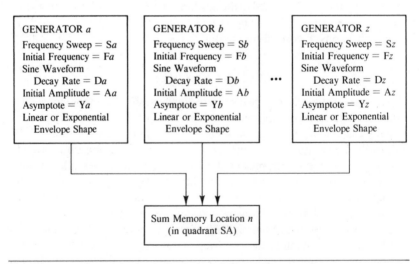

Fig. 3.2. Additive synthesis configuration

The Function of Sum Memory

The summation of a set of components is done in sum memory. The user chooses one of the 64 locations in quadrant SA as the summing point, and—by command from the host computer—directs the output of each of the generators involved to that sum memory location. These 64 locations (and a corresponding 64 for modifiers in quadrant SB) would be regarded from the viewpoint of computer architecture as an uncommonly large set of accumulators. The summing capability is provided on such a large scale in this synthesizer because it corresponds exactly to the phenomenon of mixing, which is basic to acoustic systems. The fundamental nature of this phenomenon can be obscured in analog synthesizers because of implementational difficulties.

Design Considerations for Sine Waves

The generator uses a lookup table to find the sine of an angle. How many bits wide and how many entries long should this table be? Since implementational considerations almost force the number of entries to be a power of 2, we will consider not the number of entries but the number of bits to address an entry. This number requires careful scrutiny, because each additional bit of address doubles the amount of hardware required for the table. The address size that was finally chosen is 13 bits. This results in an rms error of about 0.015%, corresponding to a signal-to-noise ratio (SNR) of about 76.5 dB.

The amount of hardware increases only linearly with the number of bits in a table entry. It proved convenient in the hardware to have that number equal to 13 also; SNR due to this quantization is about 80 dB. (The reason the SNR due to angle quantization is worse than this, when both the angle and the data entry have the same number of bits, is that the rms step size in the table is greater than 1 LSB.) This noise is built into the waveform table and can alternatively be regarded as distortion. In these terms, the total harmonic distortion of a given sinusoidal component is about 0.01%.

Except in a few special cases, the noise contribution due to the finite entry size is independent of that caused by the finite address size, so overall SNR of the sine oscillator is approximately 75 dB. Note that this is what Blesser and Kates (1978) call the signal-to-noise ratio *with signal*. Should the sine wave that results be scaled down in amplitude, the noise is scaled down too.

Frequency Design Considerations

The address that is applied to the sine table corresponds to the phase angle of the oscillator. Each sample period, the phase angle is advanced by an amount proportional to the frequency. If the phase angle is expressed as a binary fraction of a cycle, then the number which is added to it can be viewed as the frequency, expressed as a binary fraction of a cycle per sample period. How many bits should there be in the phase angle, and how many in the frequency?

Each additional bit of phase angle doubles the available frequency resolution at a given sample rate. At a 50 kHz sample rate, for example, with a 16-bit phase angle, frequency would be specified in units of approximately 0.76 Hz. (The high end of the sample-rate range was taken because resolution in terms of hertz gets worse with higher sampling rates.) At first glance, psychoacoustic information would seem to indicate that this is ample resolution, since the level of auditory pitch discrimination is never less than about 3 Hz. There is a worse problem, however, than simply resolving distinct tones. Two tones which are close in frequency will produce beats, which can be perceived in the time domain rather than in the frequency domain. A frequency resolution of 0.76 Hz means the maximum possible beat period is 1.32 sec, the next smaller one is 0.61 sec, and so on. These values were judged to be too small and too far apart. Similar problems can occur when calculating frequency values for vibrato. The number of bits actually chosen for the phase angle in this synthesizer is 20, which gives an additional factor of 16 over these examples; the resulting frequency resolution is better than 0.05 Hz.

Frequency Sweep Design Considerations

Since the only use of the frequency term is to add it to the phase angle, any more than 20 bits for frequency would seem superfluous. However, each generator has a built-in provision for frequency sweep, which bears on the number of bits in the frequency, just as the issue of frequency resolution bears on the number of bits in the phase angle. If the frequency were represented by 20 bits, the lowest rate at which it could be swept (assuming a 50 kHz sample rate, again the hard end of the scale) would be nearly 2400 Hz/sec (cycles/sec^2). This figure is quite excessive for practical glissandi and vibrati. Therefore a total of 28 bits was provided for the frequency. Only 20 bits (including sign) are needed, however, for the sweep term, since that is enough for a minimum sweep rate of about 9.3 Hz/sec and a maximum of about 465 000 Hz/sec. (The minimum is lower, and the resolution finer, at sample rates below 50 kHz.) The sweep term is added into the low-order end of the frequency term; the high-order bits of the frequency are added into the phase angle.

Amplitude Design Considerations

The ability of listeners to distinguish similar amplitudes is poorer, in quantitative terms, than their ability to distinguish frequencies. A threshold of 0.4 dB is commonly quoted, and that is a difference in amplitude of about 5%. Besides resolution to this level, however, the amplitude term of a generator must encompass a reasonable dynamic range. A size of 12 bits was chosen; this gives a set of 4096 possible instantaneous amplitude values which can be applied, within the generator, to a given oscillation. In other words, the amplitude range of an envelope is 72 dB. Several means are discussed later by which further dynamic-range scaling can be applied to a signal.

Envelope Shapes

For exponential decay, the 12-bit amplitude value comes out of an exponential table. An asymptote term, also 12 bits, is provided as well. The exponential amplitude is added to, or subtracted from, the asymptote so that any amplitude—not just 0—can be exponentially approached from above or below. The address on the exponential table is 12 bits in size as well. This is the decay coefficient. The decay coefficient must be swept, however, to cause the amplitude to rise or fall with time, and substantially more than 12 bits are needed in the decay coefficient so that it can be swept at a reasonably slow rate. In fact, 24 bits are allotted. This yields a maximum rise or fall time (assuming a sample rate of 50 kHz, since the high end of the scale is again the more difficult) of greater than 5 minutes, with 10% resolution at 33 sec, more than adequate even for *A Day in the Life*.

The synthesizer also has means to bypass the exponential lookup, using the high-order 12 bits of the decay coefficient directly as the amplitude. This permits amplitudes to be swept linearly as an alternative to exponential shape. The linear envelope shape is well known in other kinds of synthesis and was easy to implement.

Decay Rate Design Considerations

There was felt to be no need to sweep the amplitude from maximum to 0, or vice versa, in just one sample period, so the amplitude sweep term has fewer bits than the decay coefficient. It has 20 bits, meaning that the sweep between "full on" and "full off" takes at least 16 sample periods. At 18 kHz (since in this case a low sample rate is worse), this amounts to about 0.9 ms.

Envelope Modes

Generally an envelope rises or falls to a target value. In the absence of special attention, however, the decay coefficient would continue to change and would eventually overflow, causing a sudden drastic change in amplitude. To prevent this, the generator has a "sticky" mode in which, rather than overflowing, the decay coefficient sticks, or pins, at its last nonoverflow value.

A triggering facility is afforded by submodes. When these submodes are used, one generator—when its envelope overflows—will become inactive and a subsequent generator can become active. With proper choice of asymptotes, an attack-decay-sustain-release pattern (to use a simple example), employing either linear or exponential envelope segments, can be formed with a set of four generators. This is an alternative to having one generator that receives four successive commands from the computer.

Generator Shifting and Scaling

Locations in sum memory contain 20 bits (for reasons discussed later). The output of a generator is the product of a 12-bit unsigned amplitude and a 13-bit signed waveform; it has as a consequence no more than 13 significant bits, which may however be any 13 contiguous bits in the full 25-bit signed product. To fit the product into sum memory, the low-order 5 bits must be discarded; in any event they are the least likely to be significant. As a tradeoff between possibly losing more significance, and potentially overflowing when summing two or more generators into one sum memory location, the next low-order bit of the product is also discarded, and the 19-bit value that remains is added right-adjusted (with sign extended) into sum memory.

FREQUENCY-MODULATION SYNTHESIS

The frequency-modulation (FM) technique described by Chowning (1973) is another widely used synthesis method. In its most elementary form, the output of one sine generator is used to modulate the frequency of a second sine generator. More elaborate forms are also used; the modulating waveform may be more complicated—the sum of different sinusoids, for instance—and it may be used, possibly at different amplitudes, to modulate a number of different generators.

In this synthesizer, every generator has the capability of taking one term from sum memory (anywhere in quadrant SC or SD). If the generator is in an oscillatory mode, that term is used for frequency modulation. (As a consequence, any oscillator which the user does not wish to modulate must designate a source location in SC or SD that is known to contain 0, such as one for which the corresponding location of SA or SB has no active generators or modifiers adding into it.) This architecture (coupled with the ability of processing elements to scale quantities in sum memory) provides a general framework for FM configurations. Figure 3.3 shows a configuration in which two oscillators are summed and the result used to modulate a third oscillator.

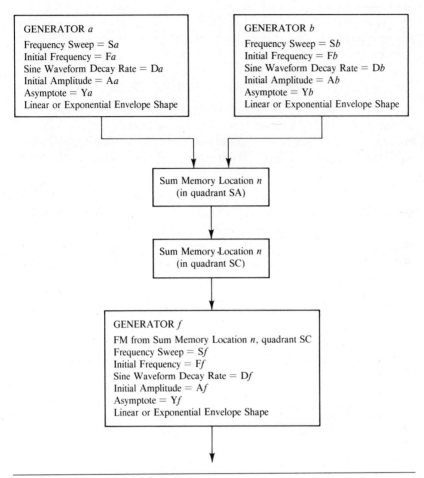

Fig. 3.3. FM synthesis configuration

Design Considerations for FM

The FM term from sum memory and the phase angle into which it is added are both 20-bit quantities, so design questions as to bit alignment do not arise. There is, however, a more subtle problem that applies especially to the elementary FM configuration. The 1-bit right shift that the output of a generator undergoes as it is added into sum memory, provided as a convenience when summing several generators, can be a drawback when that generator is being used for the FM input to another. This 1-bit shift limits the possible frequency deviation due to FM to half of full scale. For this reason, a mode bit is provided in the generator that suppresses the right shift and adds the result into sum memory left-adjusted.

SUBTRACTIVE SYNTHESIS

Subtractive synthesis is the next major technique to be considered. Its principle is to take a spectrally rich waveform and pass it through an array of filters, boosting some frequencies and attenuating others. The shape of the source waveform is often not of as much concern as the characteristics of the filters.

Excitation Waveforms

The square, sawtooth, and pulse-train waveshapes are all commonly used as source signals for subtractive synthesis. The generator can produce each one of these as alternatives to the sine wave. (These capabilities were simple to implement.) These waveshapes have a characteristic, however, which may be quite undesirable: they are not band-limited. Implicit in their sampled representation are harmonics which *fold over,* usually resulting in nonharmonic frequencies. There are some uses for this phenomenon, but there are many cases where it is unwanted.

Therefore a significant amount of hardware (including two special-purpose multipliers) is provided in the generator to create buzz waveforms, which are rich in harmonics but band-limited. For a given value of the parameter N, the buzz waveform consists of the first N harmonics of the oscillatory frequency at equal amplitude. The formula, after Winham and Steiglitz (1970), is

$$\cos(t) + \cos(2t) + \cdots + \cos(Nt) = \frac{1}{2} \frac{\sin\left[(2N + 1)\dfrac{t}{2}\right]}{\sin\left(\dfrac{t}{2}\right)} - \frac{1}{2}.$$

To prevent overflow, the resulting value is subjected to a binary right shift; the number of places is designated by a new parameter M. (This can be used to scale sine waves as well.) To keep the amount of hardware for this feature within reason, two simplifications were made in the actual implementation of the formula. First, to avoid a division operation, the division by $\sin(t/2)$ was changed to multiplication by $\csc(t/2)$. Second, the subtraction of $1/2$ was omitted; this simply means that harmonics 0 through N are summed rather than 1 through N. The resulting dc offset causes no deleterious effects in most applications. It is necessary to use a form of floating-point representation internally to maintain accuracy during the multiplication of the sine term by the cosecant.

Filter Sections

Filtering is done by modifiers. Modes are provided to simulate a resonance (pole pair), an antiresonance (zero pair), a single pole, and a single zero. Time constraints limit each modifier to two multiplications. In the 2-pole or 2-zero mode the multiplications are used for the first- and second-order feedback or feedforward coefficients; in the 1-pole or 1-zero mode, they are used for the feedback or feedforward coefficient and for an overall gain coefficient. Modifiers in these modes can be interconnected (through sum memory) to form elaborate filter configurations.

A signal that is filtered pays a price in SNR. The key issue here is the number of bits that are retained after each multiplication. Low-order product bits must be thrown away to keep the output word the same size as the input; this may entail throwing away significance as well. The amount of degradation introduced by a filter stage depends not only on the coefficient values in the filter but also on the nature of the signal put into it. Some general rules can be stated:

1. Each additional bit retained gains 6 dB of SNR.
2. The sharper the filter (the narrower its bandwidth), the worse the resulting SNR.
3. The lower the resonant frequency (as a fraction of the sample rate), the worse the SNR.
4. Sine waves are much easier to filter than white noise.

It is noteworthy that physical resonators, either acoustic or electrical, face corresponding problems: low resonant frequencies, for instance, need large vibrating bodies, large inductors or large numbers of bits.

The choice of how many bits to retain after a filter multiplication is very important, for it applies as well to the number of bits in a signal passed from one filter section to another. The number of bits chosen is therefore the word size in sum memory and in delay memory. The number should be as small as possible to minimize the hardware device count; this constraint is especially applicable in the filter multiplier itself (part of the modifier), where the amount of hardware goes up as the square of the number of bits. On the other hand, the number of bits should be made as large as possible to counteract the degradation in SNR that occurs in filtering. For instance, at a sample rate of 30 kHz a signal resembling white noise (a particularly bad example, but not an unlikely one) can lose 4 bits of significance passing through a single resonator whose resonant frequency is 1800 Hz and whose bandwidth is 800 Hz. Through a cascade of resonators, of course, the loss is even worse, though typically it is less than linear in the number of sections cascaded; it is more nearly proportional to the square root. No matter how many bits are provided, it is still an easy matter to concoct a filter that needs more; the tradeoff therefore has no hard limits. To resolve this problem, the law of marginal utility was applied to a sample of the digital filters seen in computer-music practice. The answer that resulted is 20 bits. While a smaller number, such as 18 bits, is adequate in the majority of cases, the number of important cases it rules out was judged too large to be acceptable.

A coefficient-sweep feature is incorporated in the modifier. If enabled, this adds a control term from sum memory (independent of the signal input) into one or the other coefficient in 2-pole or 2-zero mode. To accommodate practical sweep rates, the coefficients have 30 bits each; the sweep term is added in right-adjusted, and the high-order 20 bits go to the multiplier. This feature was incorporated by analogy with voltage-controlled filters.

Combining Filter Sections

A set of modifiers can be cascaded by using sum memory to pass the output of each modifier to the next. Such cascading is a typical way of forming a complex filter from resonators and antiresonators. Normally a separate sum memory location would be needed for each intermediate signal, but because cascaded filter sections are so widely used, an additional capability was added to the modifier. Under control of a mode bit, a modifier can have its output replace the contents of a location in SB rather than adding into it. Hence a cascade of modifiers can reuse the same location for successive intermediate results. In this case, however, the signal must pass through successive sections in order of increasing modifier number. Control of this capability is independent of the function a modifier is actually performing, so it can be used in many applications besides filtering. Figure 3.4 shows a typical cascade configuration in which different sum memory locations are used for intermediate results in the interests of clarity.

Another typical filter configuration comprises a number of sections in parallel. This arrangement can be accomplished simply and economically; all sections take their input from the same sum memory location and add their outputs into another common location.

The direct form of a complex filter is used much less often than the cascade and parallel forms, primarily because its SNR is substantially worse. If needed, it can be configured with an average of one sum memory location and two modifiers per pole pair or zero pair.

DELAY LINES AND REVERBERATION SYNTHESIS

The next class of synthesis techniques to be considered are those involving delay lines, including reverberation. The architectural approach taken was to

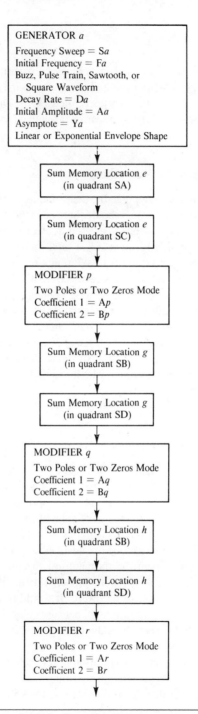

Fig. 3.4. Subtractive synthesis configuration

have a large block of storage, called *delay memory,* partitioned by the user into segments. These segments are usually, but not necessarily, distinct; each segment is accessed by a sort of memory port called a *delay unit.* Each active delay unit is coupled to the rest of the synthesizer through a modifier.

Delay Memory Design Considerations

Two architectural questions apply to the delay memory: how many bits should it have in a word; how many words should there be in the memory? The number of bits is 20, because for reasons discussed above that is the size of signals passed between processing elements. The total number of words is proportional, at a given sample rate, to the total amount of delay time that the delay memory comprises. The amount chosen was 64K words. At a 50 kHz sample rate (the high end of the scale being the most demanding), this amount corresponds to a total delay of 1.3 sec; though not overabundant, it has proven satisfactory for practical applications. At lower sample rates the same amount of memory corresponds to more time: 3.6 sec at 18 kHz, for instance. (The principal impediment to a larger amount of delay memory is in the address-arithmetic portion of the delay units, which reached a number of implementational limits simultaneously at 64K.)

Delay Unit Design Considerations

The number of delay units available was chosen to be 32. The hardware constraint here is that certain portions of the delay unit calculator, because of the speed at which they must run, increase in size proportionally to the number of delay units. In view of the total amount of delay memory available, the provision of 32 delay units has proved to be ample.

A modifier can be put into a mode that invokes a delay unit. In that mode, a parameter of the modifier identifies the delay unit to which it is connected. The alternative, to have a permanent association between modifiers and delay units, would have saved a good deal of hardware. It would have introduced a new class of programming constraint, though, because some modifiers would have special properties which others would not have. Therefore that approach was not taken.

The all-pass reverberation configuration described by Schroeder (1962) is shown in figure 3.5a. To implement this with one delay unit and one modifier, it was changed to the equivalent form shown in figure 3.5b, which accomplishes the same result with only two multiplications. This configuration can perform

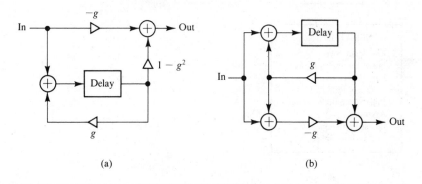

(a)　　　　　　　　　　　　　　　　　(b)

Fig. 3.5. All-pass reverberator (after Schroeder 1962)

several useful functions depending on the values given to the two gain coefficients, A and B:

$$A = -B \neq 0 \quad \text{all-pass reverberator}$$
$$A = 0, B \neq 0 \quad \text{comb filter}$$
$$A \neq 0, B = 0 \quad \text{echo}$$
$$A = B \quad = 0 \quad \text{delay line}$$

Since the modifier can read and write anywhere in the relevant quadrants of sum memory, the delay line (or reverberator, comb filter, or echo generator) is available for use as a building block in more complex reverberation structures. Many such structures have been proposed, and the development of new ones—to make the reverberation more interesting or natural-sounding in one way or another—is a continuing effort (Moorer 1979).

TABLE LOOKUP SYNTHESIS TECHNIQUES

A segment of delay memory can also be used by a delay unit as a stored table rather than a delay line. This stored table can be used to represent a mathematical function (square root, for example), a periodic waveform, or an irregular envelope. One interesting application of this capability is the synthesis technique known as *waveshaping* (Arfib 1979; LeBrun 1979; Roads 1979), in which a computed signal is mapped through a table which alters its waveshape. A simple waveshaping configuration is shown in figure 3.6. Since multiple delay units can refer to the same area of delay memory, a given waveshaping table need appear in delay memory only once to be used in shaping a number of different signals.

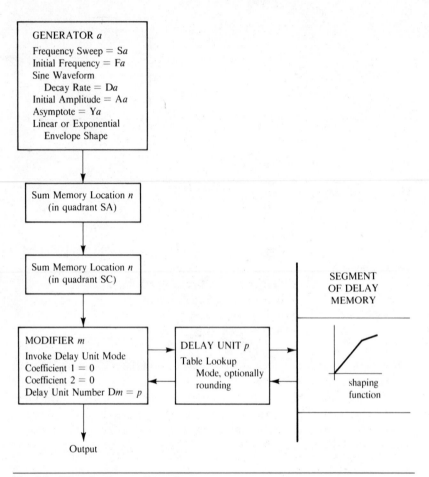

Fig. 3.6. Waveshaping configuration

A delay unit in table lookup mode takes an input from the associated modifier (which may have gotten it directly from sum memory). It shifts that input
value to the right some number of bits, and uses the shifted result as an index
into the delay unit's segment of delay memory. The number of significant bits
that remain after the shift should generally be the number of bits needed to
specify an address within the segment. This feature lets the user choose the size
of each table. In another lookup mode, the delay unit rounds the shifted index;
depending on the use of the table, this can be equivalent to adding another
address bit in terms of the resulting accuracy. If yet more accuracy is needed,

other configurations (using several modifiers, and two delay units addressing the same area of delay memory) can perform linear interpolation.

OTHER MODIFIER CAPABILITIES

Noise

The synthesizer must be able to generate something like white noise. A modifier mode is included for this purpose; it makes a uniformly distributed noise signal by the linear congruential method (Knuth 1969, pp. 155–56). All the parameters of this process can be designated by the user, either to add coloration or to ensure the independence of different noise sources. A variant mode causes the modifier to hold a given random value until triggered by an input signal.

Mixing and Modulation

Numerous modifier modes perform general signal-processing operations which are not necessarily associated with specific synthesis techniques. These include scaled mixing, amplitude modulation, and balanced modulation. In scaled mixing, a modifier takes two terms from sum memory, multiplies each by a separate gain coefficient, and adds the sum of the results into sum memory. In amplitude modulation, it takes one input as the amplitude control on the other input, and multiplies the result by an overall gain factor. In balanced modulation, the two inputs are multiplied together and then by an overall gain coefficient. All of these operations are performed with 20-bit arithmetic; therefore, as an illustration, this means that spurious components in the output of the balanced modulator are approximately 120 dB down from full scale.

Nonlinear and Conditional Operations

Various nonlinear operations are also provided, including maximum/minimum, signum, latch, threshold, and zero-crossing pulser. In the minimum or maximum mode, two inputs are each multiplied by corresponding gain coefficients and the algebraically greater or lesser result is taken. The signum mode causes an output of $+1$, 0, or -1, corresponding to input values greater than, equal to, or less than 0. A modifier in latch mode acts as a track-and-hold unit, with a signal input and a control input. The output follows the signal input, while the control input is nonzero; otherwise it holds its previous value.

A modifier in threshold mode also takes a signal input and a control input, and acts as a conditional element. Its output is zero when the control input (after multiplication by a signed scale factor) is less than the threshold value (a parameter of the modifier); otherwise its output follows the signal input, multiplied by a gain coefficient. In the zero-crossing pulser mode, the output is zero except when the value of the input signal becomes, or crosses, zero.

These modes are provided because of their use in either computer-based signal processing or analog synthesizers. Some effort was exerted to generalize the typical operations: the maximum/minimum operations in this design, for instance, are generalizations of rectification and clipping.

SPEECH SYNTHESIS

Digital synthesis of speech is a well-established field that encompasses a variety of competing approaches. The simplest technique has a stored waveform for each word; these waveforms are played back in the proper order to form the desired utterance. This approach is quite limited in subject matter (because of memory requirements) and in naturalness. More advanced speech synthesis techniques attempt to mimic the human vocal system. An excitation waveform, similar to that produced by the vocal cords for a voiced sound or to white noise for an unvoiced sound, is passed through a set of filter sections which are analogous to the vocal tract.

An underlying aspect of the research in this area is to develop differential equations which accurately describe the acoustic phenomena that take place in the production of human speech. It is interesting to speculate as to what state digital music synthesis would be in today had it followed the same approach. Would there be special-purpose hardware to solve the equations of motion for a violin body?

Typical excitation functions for voiced speech are the pulse train (not necessarily band-limited!), a train of raised cosine pulses, and a train of asymmetrical triangular pulses; and for unvoiced speech, white noise. All of these signals are easily produced in this synthesizer. One way to make the asymmetrical triangle pulse train is to use the envelope triggering facility. This approach employs one generator that determines the repetition rate, and two subsequent generators (with phase angles standing still at 90°) whose envelopes form the ramp up and the ramp down.

The speech excitation waveform is passed through a network of filters. Some approaches simply use a cascade of resonators (and possibly antiresonators); others use a series of lattice-filter sections. Because each lattice section has two outputs, it requires a pair of modifiers.

All these speech synthesis algorithms are straightforwardly and fully supported by the synthesizer. The accuracy provided is far more than necessary, and the computational rate is sufficient for as many as 16 voices speaking at once.

INPUT AND OUTPUT OF SIGNALS

The input and output of signals are vital capabilities, even though these operations use only a small fraction of the hardware in the synthesizer. Both input and output can be accomplished in two domains: analog and digital.

A generator can be put in a mode in which it does not generate a signal, but rather acts as a pathway from sum memory to a DAC (*DAC mode*); from an ADC to sum memory (*ADC mode*); from sum memory to the memory of the host computer (*write-data mode*); or from the memory of the host computer to sum memory (*read-data mode*).

Analog Signal I/O

Plug-in card slots are provided for 16 channels of analog I/O. Each channel is either a digital-to-analog converter (DAC) for output or an analog-to-digital converter (ADC) for input. All 20 bits taken from sum memory appear on a DAC channel connector, and all 20 bit positions going into sum memory appear on an ADC channel connector. The synthesizer can therefore accommodate converters of any precision up to 20 bits. The cost of a converter increases as more than a linear power of the number of bits, so the tradeoff of accuracy against expense must be analyzed carefully. This analysis was done during the initial design phase for the DACs, and more recently for the ADCs; in each case 14 bits was chosen as a standard value. The interface to the analog cards was deliberately kept simple and well-defined, so that converters of different accuracy can be provided with a comparatively modest amount of effort, or existing converters can be connected to the interface. As a further alternative, converters which are already part of the host computer system can be connected by software with the digital I/O streams of the synthesizer, described below.

The DACs require deglitching; both the DACs and the ADCs require low-pass filtering of the analog signal. These processes are performed on the analog cards. The low-pass filtering is to remove components with frequencies above one-half the sampling rate. To allow for transition from the passband to the stopband, filter response is typically designed to start falling off at around 40% or 45% of the sampling frequency. A complication arises in this synthesizer because the sample rate can be varied in fine steps over a wide range. Two provisions were made for dealing with this. First, a programmable analog low-pass filter was included on each channel: by computer command, any of four prewired breakpoint frequencies can be selected. The degree of approximation to the desired breakpoint that this entails, while rather coarse, has proved to be generally acceptable. The Butterworth configuration is used, rather than one with a sharper cutoff, in order to minimize the amount of violence done to the phase characteristics of the signal. Second, a mode is provided in which the low-pass filter is bypassed altogether; external equipment can then be used to perform whatever filtering is desired.

Correction for the aperture error of the DAC, which manifests itself as a mild high-frequency rolloff, is not included on the analog cards. In cases where this correction is needed, it can easily be performed as part of the digital processing in the synthesizer.

Digital Signal I/O

The read-data and write-data modes provide several important benefits. The synthesizer can be used to process previously digitized natural sound, or sound synthesized by other means, or to combine that sound with the results of its own synthesis. The output of the synthesizer can be saved in digital form, for subsequent playback or transmission without the degradation inherent in analog recording and transmission techniques. Also, the synthesizer can be used to advantage for a synthesis task which is beyond its real-time capabilities. For instance, the user can employ 500 generators and 250 modifiers by running the synthesis in two passes: intermediate results are written to computer memory during the first pass, and read back during the second.

Some of these capabilities have their counterparts in the tape studio, but now these can be performed at computer speeds and without the progressive degeneration of successive tape copies. Other capabilities provided by digital I/O are unique to the digital realm. Inclusion of the read-data and write-data modes in the architecture of this synthesizer followed naturally from experience with other data-processing equipment.

COMMANDS

Synthesis is directed by a stream of commands from computer memory. Each command alters one parameter of a given processing element; the typical meaning of a command is "Set parameter P of generator (or modifier or delay unit) number N to the value V." Commands are performed during the update ticks at the end of each sample period; generally one update tick is required per command. The command stream must be strictly in order of the actions to be taken. To synchronize command performance properly with the passage of time, a special command named *linger* directs the synthesizer not to perform further commands until the end of a particular numbered sample period.

Command Rates

Some architectural decisions hinge on the question of the rate at which the synthesizer must be able to perform commands. This question, in fact, asks for two different numbers: the peak rate, or how many parameters must be updated in one sample period; and the average rate, or how many parameters must be updated over a long period of time (say 1 sec).

During the design phase, the opinion was heard from an academic quarter that it was necessary to be able to update all the parameters of the synthesizer in the update portion of one sample period. Since the parameters number in the thousands, such a requirement would have had a severe impact on the amount of hardware. For this machine to be feasible, it was necessary to have a much lower limit. (It is in fact possible in this synthesizer to change all the parameters in the time between two samples, by performing the synthesis out of real time and using the write-data stream. A *stop* command is available to interrupt the synthesis following a designated sample period.)

Commands must be fetched from the memory of the host computer, which in general cannot provide them at a rate of one command per tick. Therefore there is a command buffer in the synthesizer. When an update period begins, first all the commands in the buffer are performed, one after the other; then, at a slower rate, the buffer is refilled from computer memory. As each command is taken from memory, if the synthesizer is still in the update period the command can be performed. Hence the peak rate of command execution depends first on the buffer size, and second on the number of update ticks provided in excess of the buffer size in relation to the speed of the computer memory. Expansion of the command buffer is comparatively costly, as a result of the speed at which it must operate, and the size of 28 words was initially chosen. Recent improvements in memory technology have permitted this to be increased to 60. There is one case which received special treatment. In additive synthesis, the initial onset of a note may require a large number of generators to start synchronously. (It is much less likely that they will have to stop synchronously.) Two generator modes were provided—*pause mode* and *wait mode*—for this purpose. A single command starts all generators in pause mode, and a different command starts all those in wait mode.

The question of average rate is whether, over the long term, the computer system can keep up with the synthesizer's appetite for commands. Since the synthesizer is often—in fact, usually—performing a linger command, waiting for the right time to resume command execution, the average rate is much lower than the peak rate. Analysis from several viewpoints led to the estimate that average rates would be between 100 and 10 000 commands per second, with the geometric mean of 1000 as a typical value. These rates* indicate that the host computer could easily keep up with the synthesizer by reading commands from a mass storage device, such as a disk, but at least in some cases could not compile the commands in real time (Moorer 1981). Measurements of command rates in actual use have shown very good agreement with the original estimates.

Command Format

A 32-bit format is used for commands. This includes 20 bits for the typical parameter value V, up to 8 bits to designate the processing element number N, and the remainder to identify the specific parameter P. A few parameters are larger than 20 bits and require two successive commands to specify the full value; but there are special provisions to ensure that the entire parameter will be updated in the same tick. In cases where several related parameters comprise less than 20 bits, they can sometimes be given as fields of the same command. The size of 32 bits was chosen for compatibility with the great majority of possible host computers.

Provisions for External Devices

There are various tasks which one might want to be controlled in synchronism with musical synthesis. These include the dramatic—operating the stage lights, for instance; the acoustic, such as changing loudspeaker patches; and the prosaic, like starting and stopping a tape recorder. Performing these tasks directly from the host computer could have problems of synchronization because the synthesizer uses its own precise time base. To preclude such a problem the synthesizer has two digital output registers, as well as commands to load them; the users can attach whatever equipment they wish to these outputs.

DIAGNOSTIC AIDS

The issues of reliability and maintainability can easily be overlooked in specifying what is, in effect, a musical instrument. From the viewpoint of the data-processing industry, however, they are crucial issues and deserve a great deal of attention. In a machine of this size (2500 integrated circuits) the designer must

---

*Experience has shown, however, that high peak rates require special attention in order to prevent the synthesizer from "running out" of commands.—*Ed.*

prepare for the possibility of an occasional failure. Identification of the actual component at fault can be a challenging task. The fact that the synthesizer is a computer peripheral, however, offers the hope of computer-aided fault diagnosis. To fulfill this hope requires significant amounts of both hardware in the synthesizer and software in the computer. Some 10% of the synthesizer components take no part in signal processing but are strictly for diagnostic functions. Programs comprising about 70 000 computer instructions were written to use the diagnostic hardware. These diagnostic facilities have been used extensively, both during initial checkout and later in the field.

SPECIAL-PURPOSE OR GENERAL-PURPOSE?

There is one reason for using special-purpose computational hardware: speed. By the same token, given a computational task to be performed at high speed, the hardware can be minimized by tailoring its architecture to the purpose at hand. Digital music synthesis, however, is a rapidly developing field; some of the algorithms to be performed are well known, while others are still being discovered. This situation suggests a synthesizer architecture which is basically general-purpose but which contains various special features to improve the performance of well-established algorithms. The Systems Concepts synthesizer fits this description.

The generators have more of a special-purpose appearance than the modifiers, since the generators are optimized to create large numbers of frequency-modulated sine (or buzz) waveforms and exponential (or linear) envelopes. As a side effect, the data path from sum memory, through a generator, and back to sum memory is only 13 bits wide at one point. Within this limitation, which is tolerable in many cases, the generator can actually be used for various general operations including the following:

- Scaling a value in sum memory
- Generating a ramp
- Applying an envelope to a signal in sum memory
- Clipping a signal

Each of these operations can of course be performed with 20-bit accuracy by a modifier. It is fair, in a sense, that a generator does the task with less accuracy, since generators constitute a more abundant resource than modifiers.

The modifiers possess special capabilities also, particularly to expedite filtering and reverberation. They are, however, more general in intent than the generators, as shown by their following properties:

- Modifier data paths are a full 20 bits wide.
- Modifiers can combine or compare two inputs.
- Modifiers can perform conditional operations.

Hardware Savings

The amount of hardware that is saved (or, equivalently, the amount of performance that is gained) by fitting the design to the purpose can be estimated in several ways. One approach is to write a program that simulates the synthesizer (performing a typical synthesis) on a computer with a comparable amount of hardware. This approach results in a factor of roughly 100, the computer being that much slower. If one imagines redesigning the computer somewhat, moving hardware from features that are not needed to special features that are needed, perhaps a factor of 3 could be gained back. This would put the disadvantage of the redesigned general-purpose machine at about a factor of 30. (Some of this is because many calculations are being done to more precision than necessary.)

An alternative approach starts with the synthesizer and adds hardware as necessary to make the architecture like that of a typical computer. To do this, keeping the tick time unchanged, would increase the hardware by close to a factor of 2. The performance of such a machine, though, doing a typical synthesis task, would be about 12 times slower. The reason for this slower speed is that the general-purpose machine can have only one operation in progress at a time. The synthesizer as built, due to pipelining, has eight operations in the generator, eight in the modifier, three in the delay unit, one in delay memory, and possibly one in the computer interface, all going on at once. The concept of pipelining conflicts in various regards with that of individually programmed instructions.

Each of these analyses gives a factor in the range between 20 and 30 as the cost of general-purpose user-programmable architecture. Even if this could be brought down by another factor of 2, a machine ten times larger than the present one would still be required to attain the same performance.

SPEED AND CAPACITY

There remain to be discussed the reasons behind the tick time (195 ns), the number of generators supported (256), the number of modifiers supported

(128), and the size of a sum memory quadrant (64 words). An implementation consideration here is that the random-access memory (RAM) chips to be used were available only in certain sizes: 16 256, or 4096 words. The more words a chip holds, the slower it is; the 4096-word device used, in particular, takes well over 400 ns for a cycle.

A tick time on the order of 200 ns is quite typical of the clocked TTL logic that the synthesizer is made of. As an example, Systems Concepts had from an earlier project a design for a 20-bit-by-20-bit two's-complement multiplier running at that speed. It was therefore reasonable to assume that each of the multipliers in the synthesizer would produce one result each 200 ns (or so) tick. The tick time does not limit the total amount of calculation a generator or modifier can do, since pipeline stages can be added as necessary. The actual tick time of 195 ns was chosen because it is a multiple of 3 (which offered some minor implementational benefits) and so that 256 ticks (a round number in binary) could be accomplished in $20\mu s$ (a round number in decimal).

How Many Generators?

The generator has three distinct multipliers: two in the buzz generator and one at the output to multiply the waveform by the envelope. Those in the buzz generator have numerous peculiarities, so the provision of three separate hardware multipliers was strongly indicated. This being the case, it became feasible without an overwhelming amount of pipelining to make the generator calculator run at an average rate of one generator per tick.

The performance requirement was regarded as follows. To mimic the sound of a bowed instrument by additive synthesis appeared to take 20 or 30 generators per sounding string. Consider the string quartet, permitting some bass strings to sound after being bowed and allowing for double stops; this means about seven strings could be sounding at a time. The total number of generators indicated is between 140 and 210. The smallest power of 2 that accommodates this number is 256; generator control memory could very conveniently be implemented with 256-word RAMs; and at 195 ns per generator the string quartet could be synthesized at a sample rate of about 30 kHz.

How Many Modifiers?

The resonator and antiresonator (as well as various other modifier modes) require two multiplications. Since the multiplier involved had to be large (20 by 20), duplicating it was unattractive. Therefore each modifier was given two ticks.

Synthesizing the string quartet by subtractive techniques was judged to involve a small number of generators for the strings and about 15 to 25 modifiers per instrument for the body resonances. This indicates a total modifier count between 80 and 100. The smallest adequate power of 2 is 128; most of the control memory of a modifier is for a pair of 20-bit running terms and a pair of 30-bit coefficients; and because two ticks are available, these could be fit into a 256-by-20 memory for the running terms and a 256-by-30 memory for the coefficients. At the rate of one modifier every 390 ns, the string quartet could be performed at a 30 kHz sample rate.

How Much Sum Memory?

Because of its speed requirements the sum memory had to be made out of 16-word RAMs, so any increase in sum memory size would require a corresponding increase in its chip count. The choice of 64 words per quadrant provides a location for each two modifiers in each of quadrants SB and SD, assuming all modifiers are used. Since some modifiers will be adding into the same location (in scaled mixing operations, for instance, and parallel filter configurations), since cascaded modifiers can reuse the same location, and since most applications do not use all the modifiers, the provision of 64 locations is generally satisfactory. It is not extremely generous, but any increase would have made the most difficult part of the implementation—sum memory—even more difficult. There are also 64 words in each of quadrants SA and SC, so there are four generators per location. This seems even more limiting; but it was expected that if large numbers of generators were in use, they would be summed immediately into a smaller number of results. The amount provided has proved acceptable in practice.

CONCLUSIONS

The question is often asked why this synthesizer is so big. A better question would be why it is so small. As catalogs of recorded music indicate, listeners strongly prefer polyphonic works to monophonic ones; and among polyphonic works, they prefer those of orchestral dimensions. The number of instruments these works require is well in excess of the real-time capacity of this synthesizer.

This is especially clear in view of the amount of computation needed even for a single sound of subtlety and richness. Techniques have been found to save computation—FM synthesis is an outstanding example—and more of these will be found in the future. But as these techniques become understood, they too will be applied in larger and larger numbers. Though the capacity of the Systems Concepts synthesizer is large, its limits have already been reached. In an increasing number of cases, its capabilities are close to the minimum needed for serious work.

REFERENCES

Arfib, D. 1979. Digital synthesis of complex spectra by means of multiplication of non-linear distorted sine waves. *Journal of the Audio Engineering Society* 27(10):757–68.

Blesser, B., and J. M. Kates. 1978. Digital processing in audio signals. In A. V. Oppenheim, ed. *Applications of digital signal processing.* Englewood Cliffs, N. J.: Prentice-Hall.

Chowning, John M. 1973. The synthesis of complex audio spectra by means of frequency modulation. *Journal of the Audio Engineering Society* 21(7): 526–34. Reprinted in Curtis Roads and John Strawn, eds. 1985. *Foundations of computer music.* Cambridge: MIT Press.

Grey, John M. 1975. An exploration of musical timbre. Ph.D. dissertation, Department of Psychology, Stanford University. Department of Music Report STAN-M-2.

Knuth, Donald E. 1969. *The art of computer programming.* Vol. 2: Seminumerical algorithms. Reading, Mass.: Addison-Wesley.

LeBrun, Marc. 1979. Digital waveshaping synthesis. *Journal of the Audio Engineering Society* 27(4):250–66.

Moorer, James A. 1977. Signal processing aspects of computer music—a survey. *Proceedings of the IEEE* 65(8):1108–37. Revised and updated version in John Strawn, ed. 1985. *Digital audio signal processing: An anthology.* Los Altos, Calif.: Kaufmann.

Moorer, James A. 1979. About this reverberation business. *Computer Music Journal* 3(2):13–28. Reprinted in Curtis Roads and John Strawn, eds. *Foundations of computer music.* Cambridge: MIT Press.

Moorer, James A. 1981. Synthesizers I have known and loved. *Computer Music Journal* 5(1):4–12.

Roads, Curtis. 1979. A tutorial on non-linear distortion or waveshaping synthesis. *Computer Music Journal* 3(2):29–34. Revised and updated version in Curtis Roads and John Strawn, eds. 1985. *Foundations of computer music.* Cambridge: MIT Press.

Samson, Peter R. 1980. A general-purpose digital synthesizer. *Journal of the Audio Engineering Society* 28(3):106–13.

Schroeder, Manfred R. 1962. Natural sounding artificial reverberation. *Journal of the Acoustical Society of America* 10(3):219–23.

Winham, G., and K. Steiglitz. 1970. Input generators for digital sound synthesis. *Journal of the Acoustical Society of America* 47:665–66.

4

THE FRMBOX—A MODULAR DIGITAL MUSIC SYNTHESIZER

F. Richard Moore

Digital music synthesizers have the potential to become the
most malleable of musical instruments because, like computers, they can produce virtually any sound that can come
from loudspeakers. In fact, the distinction between digital
synthesizers and computers may often be moot, since synthesizers are just highly specialized computers. Specializa-
tion in machine architecture allows music synthesizers to
compute dozens or hundreds of times faster than typical
unadorned computers, allowing them to be used as real-time
musical instruments.

An interesting aspect of music synthesis lies in the area of identifying machine architectures that allow both efficient computation and time-varying control of the musical parameters of a sound. Music is inherently a parallel process, often requiring the specification, fine control, synthesis, distribution, and modification of several distinct sounds at once. And even though desired human-machine interactions often lie at the edge of current technological possibilities, music synthesis offers a unique advantage as a testing ground for processing architectures and control structures: it is often possible to evaluate the success of a given test strategy merely by listening with a trained musical ear. Processing errors such as arithmetic overflow or inadequate precision often will induce characteristic distortions into the sound output, and the response to control signals can be determined within perceptual limits by improvisation. Although not all processing or control errors may be found in this way, this debugging tool is not commonly available in any equivalent form.

The potential of digital music synthesis is still largely untapped, as the technology needed to realize computer music techniques in real time has existed for only a few years. Successful machines have been built by Alles (1977), Alles and diGiugno (1977), Alonso et al. (1976), Samson (1980, 1985), and others, but these designs represent only a bare beginning. As a kind of brief case study, I will describe a digital synthesizer built as part of my graduate research at Stanford University (Moore 1977a; Moorer 1977). This machine represents what I believe to be a particularly simple and flexible solution to the problem of designing a machine of relatively unpredictable function. The machine described here has been called—among other things—the FRMbox (pronounced "firmbox"). It was designed and built under the auspices of Stanford's Center for Computer Research in Music and Acoustics (CCRMA) during the 1976-77 academic year. It is currently on loan to the Computer Audio Research Laboratory within the Center for Music Experiment at the University of California, San Diego (UCSD).

DESIGN GOALS

The FRMbox was intended to provide a convenient hardware structure for ongoing research in machine architectures for real-time sound synthesis and processing. It was *not* intended, for example, as a prototype for a commercial music synthesizer, nor as a production machine optimized around a given set of known functions such as FM synthesis or digital filtering, even though it might serve these purposes very well. Rather, the machine was designed to act as a superstructure for experimenting with digital signal processing architectures, without reference to what these processes might be. Development of the

FRMbox was an attempt to implement a machine of unknown—or at least unspecified—signal processing function.

A further objective was to obtain a simple structure that could grow or shrink according to the needs of the processing task at hand. To achieve this, it should be possible to interlink several machines as needed if the processing requirements exceed the power of a single structure. At the same time, it was desired to make modularity a goal even within a single structure, so that the machine could be debugged and evaluated as each piece was built, rather than only after the entire construction was complete.

Finally, it was decided at the outset that the machine was to be controlled by a computer separate from the machine structure. This decision to build a specialized computer peripheral, rather than a complete stand-alone system, was partly a matter of convenience and partly a choice based on the desirability of not tying the signal processing structure to that of any particular sequential computer or microprocessor.

Thus, a complete music synthesis system would consist of considerably more than the FRMbox alone: it would contain, minimally, the synthesizer itself, a computer to control it (of more-or-less arbitrary choice), a set of interactive control devices such as keyboards, knobs, foot pedals and the like connected to the computer, and a set of loudspeakers and microphones for transducing sound into and out of the digital-to-analog and analog-to-digital converters connected to the synthesizer.

GROOVE

All of the above facilities existed as part of the now-defunct GROOVE system which I developed with Max Mathews and others at Bell Laboratories in the early 1970s (Mathews and Moore 1970) except that the GROOVE synthesizer was analog instead of digital. Part of the basic notion of GROOVE was to separate the acoustic waveform level of signal processing from the control signal level, since computers of that time (and modern ones as well!) could keep up with the control signals in real time but not with the audio signals. This separation allowed the computer to provide a great deal of real-time intelligent service in support of generating the control signals—a kind of real-time compositional and improvisatory aid to the system user. The GROOVE system computer could be used as a simple translator between the real-time interactive inputs and the synthesizer (a more-or-less "transparent" mode), or it might generate the entire composition on the fly, under interactive control of compositional parameters such as tempo, note density, pitch range, etc., via control knobs. The GROOVE computer also maintained files of sampled control functions in a conveniently editable form, and a very useful display which allowed one to use the stored time function files as "scores" which could be modified in real time. A few dozen simultaneous time functions could be handled at sampling rates of 100 to 200 samples per second; this rate was determined to be adequate to describe most actions that a human performer might take at a knob or other control device.

By obviating the need for the control computer to take part in the details of the sound synthesis, GROOVE provided an enormously powerful and flexible compositional control structure in real time. At the same time, nothing prevented the computer from being involved in any audio signal processing that did not require much in the way of real-time decision making. For example, a GROOVE software subsystem was built which allowed the computer to automatically calibrate the analog oscillators, which were constantly drifting and going out of tune. This automatic calibration was accomplished by using a combination of an analog-to-digital converter and a pitch detection algorithm: the computer would successively "try out" different control values in order to determine which ones resulted in the desired oscillator tunings.

This digression is not intended merely to extoll the virtues of the GROOVE system—although it had many virtues to extoll—but to point out the precise merit of placing control and acoustic signal processes into separate, parallel computer partitions. Computers can provide a very useful source of real-time control on the scale of human time perception. During the so-called "length of the present" (about 1/30 sec), a typical computer might perform 30 000 operations. This is the principle upon which timesharing rests, and many real-time tasks such as factory process control require only occasional adjustment by computer speed standards in order to seem under continuous control to a human observer. Only a modest amount of computing, however, may be done on the time scale of the acoustic waveform. Rather than sacrificing the richness of the GROOVE control structure in order to achieve digital synthesis of the sounds, it seems reasonable to retain this structure, and to simply replace the analog synthesizer with a digital one.

Implicit in this choice is the decision to separate the control and audio data streams within the synthesizer itself. This allows the synthesizer to run continuously, as would an analog synthesizer, with little or no need to multiplex commands and audio signals. Of course, at some level, control and audio signals must be equivalent or at least compatible in order to allow such processes as scaling and modulation.

OVERVIEW OF THE ARCHITECTURE

The basic structure of the FRMbox is shown in figure 4.1. A control unit is connected to two sets of eight data registers: the module input registers (MI0

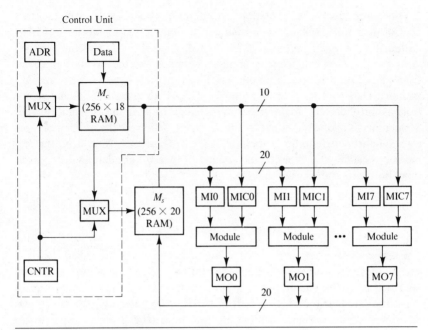

Fig. 4.1. Overview of the FRMbox architecture

through MI7) and the module output registers (MO0 through MO7). Separate unidirectional buses with 20 parallel data bits are used for the data input and output connections. Also, the control unit provides control information to the modules via a third unidirectional bus dedicated to this purpose. This bus is 10 bits wide and is connected to eight control registers (MIC0 through MIC7)— one associated with each module input register. In this way the control unit is able to pass, to each module, a piece of data together with an associated piece of control information. The control information may serve to identify the "type" of data with which it is associated so that the module can take appropriate action, such as storing the data in a local memory or processing it in some specific way; it is often possible to think of the control information as a kind of "operation code" associated with the data, although the interpretation of this code is determined strictly by the module that receives it, and not by the control unit or the data itself. A fourth unidirectional bus (not shown) provides common timing and synchronization signals to the modules for their optional use. No particular timing constraints are imposed on the internal operations of the modules. The input/output operation timing, however, is rigid and predetermined: each module is "visited" in ascending numerical order on a fixed schedule.

In order to discuss the visitation procedure, it is necessary to note that the control unit itself contains two separate, random-access memories (RAMs) called the *signal interchange memory* (M_s—see fig. 4.1) and the *control memory* (M_c). Data read from the M_s memory appears on the module input bus. Data placed on the module output bus appears at the input of this same M_s memory. Data read from the M_c memory is used both to drive the module control bus and alternately to provide address information for the M_s memory. The M_s memory is addressed either by this arbitrary data from the M_c memory, or by a synchronous counter, labeled CNTR in figure 4.1. Similarly, the M_c memory is addressed either by the counter or by arbitrary data in the control input buffer registers (ADR and DATA).

MODULE VISITATION

The sequence of events in a module visitation can now be described. During each of these visitation periods, a predetermined, sequential address is generated by the CNTR counter, and an arbitrary address value is read from control memory M_c. During the first part of the module visitation, this arbitrary address is applied to signal memory M_s, causing it to be read at an appropriate location. The data so obtained is placed onto the module input bus and clocked into the proper module input register. Simultaneously, a portion of the data which had been obtained from M_c is placed on the module control bus and clocked into the corresponding module control register. The second part of each visitation consists of storing the data from the module output register into the M_s memory at the location specified by the CNTR counter. This is accomplished via the module output bus and the two-way multiplexer at the address input of M_s. While this second part of the visitation is occurring, arbitrary data can be written into the M_c memory at an arbitrary location, thus allowing it to be updated at "visitation speed" if so desired.

Modules are visited in numerical order: first module 0, then module 1, and so on, through module 7. Then module 0 is revisited, module 1 again, and so on again. The amount of time between module visitations is fixed and represents one of the basic characteristic times associated with module operations; it is referred to as the *module service period* T_{ms}. Obviously, if a given module is designed to process digital signals, and the process can be carried out in a time less than or equal to T, then the module can always produce the result corresponding to the input received during the previous visitation whenever it is serviced by the control unit. If the module requires a time greater than T to perform its task, then the module designer has at least two options: either the module can be pipelined, or the module may simply provide valid output only at every n^{th} visitation. Pipelining is usually both possible and desirable, although it generally increases the complexity of the module.

CONTROL UNIT MEMORIES

Before discussing further considerations for the module designer, however, let's look into the control and signal memories, M_c and M_s, in a bit more detail (see figure 4.2). Since the modules are visited in numerical order, and since module outputs are written into sequential locations of M_s, this means that $M_s[0]$ will always contain the value found in MO0 during the first visitation to module 0; similarly $M_s[1]$ will contain the data found in MO1 during the first

A	V	M	←20 bits→ Contents of M_s	←18 bits→ Contents of M_c		
				←5 b→ V_{in}	←3 b→ M_{in}	←10 b→ CB_{in}
0	0	0	output of $M0V31$	V_{in}	M_{in}	CB_{in} for $M0V0$
1	0	1	output of $M1V31$	V_{in}	M_{in}	CB_{in} for $M1V0$
2	0	2	output of $M2V31$	V_{in}	M_{in}	CB_{in} for $M2V0$
3	0	3	output of $M3V31$	V_{in}	M_{in}	CB_{in} for $M3V0$
4	0	4	output of $M4V31$	V_{in}	M_{in}	CB_{in} for $M4V0$
5	0	5	output of $M5V31$	V_{in}	M_{in}	CB_{in} for $M5V0$
6	0	6	output of $M6V31$	V_{in}	M_{in}	CB_{in} for $M6V0$
7	0	7	output of $M7V31$	V_{in}	M_{in}	CB_{in} for $M7V0$
8	1	0	output of $M0V0$	V_{in}	M_{in}	CB_{in} for $M0V1$
9	1	1	output of $M1V0$	V_{in}	M_{in}	CB_{in} for $M1V1$
10	1	2	output of $M2V0$	V_{in}	M_{in}	CB_{in} for $M2V1$
⋮	⋮	⋮	⋮	⋮	⋮	⋮
253	31	5	output of $M5V30$	V_{in}	M_{in}	CB_{in} for $M5V31$
254	31	6	output of $M6V30$	V_{in}	M_{in}	CB_{in} for $M6V31$
255	31	7	output of $M7V30$	V_{in}	M_{in}	CB_{in} for $M7V31$

Fig. 4.2. Address maps of the M_s and M_c memories in the FRMbox control unit

visitation to module 1, etc. $M_s[7]$ will contain the data found in the second visitation of MO0, since modules are just revisited in the same order during each set of visitations.

Eventually, of course, the M_s memory will become full, and the number of times an individual module is visited before this happens determines the number of distinct operations that one module can perform during the calculation of one sample of the acoustic waveform by the FRMbox. Schottky TTL technology available at the time of the FRMbox's design dictated the following values as a convenient set of timing parameters: if both M_s and M_c were made to be 256 locations long, the choice of 8 as a number of modules (determined largely by bus load and drive capabilities of the integrated circuits) fixes the number of module operations per sample at 32. Increasing the number of modules to 16 is conceivable, with a corresponding reduction of module operations per sample to 16—the choice between more operations and fewer modules vs more modules with fewer operations per sample seems to be determined primarily by how the module operations themselves are conceived. More complex modules might require fewer operations; simpler modules are likely to require more operations in order to accomplish a given signal processing or synthesis task. Initially, at least, it seemed wise to proceed in the direction of simpler modules; hence I chose a 32-by-8 design.

The remaining choice—the choice of visitation period that directly determines the sampling rate—was largely constrained by the memory speed. It turns out that a visitation period just under 120 ns would yield a sampling rate of 32 768 samples per second. Since this sampling rate is a power of 2, certain advantage can be taken of the fact that the increment necessary for a given frequency using the table lookup oscillator algorithm (Moore 1977b) is numerically equal to the frequency scaled by a power of 2, depending on the length of the table (which must also be a power of 2), since

$$\text{Increment} = \frac{\text{frequency} \times \text{sampling rate}}{\text{table length}}$$

This choice of sampling rate both simplifies the calculation of the increment values to simple binary shifts instead of high-precision multiplies, and also provides a reasonable audio bandwidth.

The memory maps of M_c and M_s are then as shown in figure 4.2. A refers to an 8-bit memory address, V is a visitation number between 0 and 31, M is a module number between 0 and 7, and CB is a set of control (operation code) bits. At a given address A, M_s contains the output of a given visitation of a given module, and M_c contains the address from which the input of that same module is to be read, allowing modules and module functions to be linked together into processing networks. M_c also contains a 10-bit operation code for each visitation to each module.

It is possible to think of each module in terms of its 32 operations per sample as if there were 32 virtual modules operating simultaneously. For example, an oscillator module could generate 32 independent signals, and each calculation for each virtual oscillator could occur in a separate operation mode under control of the control bits. This is, of course, one of the great advantages of time-multiplexed digital circuits: a single circuit may be rather expensive and/or complex, but that cost and/or complexity is divided by the number of times it can be time-multiplexed in order to get the cost/complexity *per oscillator function*. Even if an oscillator module for a digital synthesizer costs, say, $3000, time multiplexing by a factor of 32 would bring its cost *per oscillator function* to under $100, which compares very favorably with analog technology costs (assuming, of course, that one happens to need 32 oscillators or thereabouts on a fairly regular basis).

I/O

This simple structure for the control unit satisfies all the design goals mentioned earlier. A straightforward programmed I/O interface allows the control computer to write in randomly selected locations of the M_c memory in the control unit as fast as once every 120 ns, if desired. Thus the entire contents of M_c, which determines simultaneously the effective interconnection of virtual module operations and the opcode or mode for each of these operations, could be entirely rewritten during a single sample period by a very fast direct-memory transfer, if so desired (and if the control computer's memory is sufficiently fast). Digital signal I/O is done entirely by the modules themselves: typically module 0 is dedicated to analog-to-digital and/or digital-to-analog conversion. Up to 32 simultaneous signals can be mixed and/or distributed among an arbitrary number of audio channels (up to 32) by module 0 operations. The control computer may be used to supply an arbitrary number of digital signals via module 0 as well, thus allowing it to generate sound control parameters as well as interconnection and opcode control data along independent pathways. Modules may have one or more inputs or outputs simply by masquerading as multiple modules.

Finally, a control unit may be interconnected with other control units in the manner shown in figure 4.3, which illustrates a 32-channel, full-duplex interconnection possibility. Any input which is selected for module 7 on one machine appears as the output of module 7 on the other, allowing two-way communication of up to 32 signals in each direction. Both control units CU1

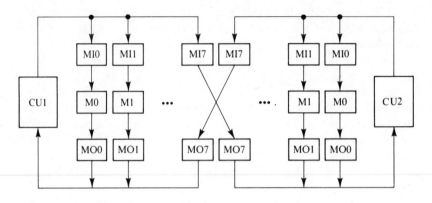

Fig. 4.3.　Interconnection of two FRMbox control units

and CU2 would need to be synchronized in order for this scheme to work, but such synchronization is relatively simple to achieve. An arbitrary number of control units may also be interconnected in several ways: one of the simplest is a "ring" of control units which would make a careful partitioning of the signal processing task desirable, but which would have the advantage of ease of modification.

DESIGN CONSIDERATIONS FOR MODULES

The module functions themselves are, of course, the determinants of the actual function of the synthesizer. Several general types of modules are conveniently realizable within the FRMbox structure.

A general formulation of the function of a single-input, single-output module with k control bits is

$$y \leftarrow M_c(x),$$

where y is the module output, x is the input, c is a k-bit control code (there are 2^k such codes), and $m_j(\cdot)$, $0 \leq j < c$, is one of the different specifiable module operations. With 10 control bits, then, each module has a repertory of up to 1024 distinguishable operations. A two-input module, by virtue of its access to 20 control bits, has a potential vocabulary of over 1 million operations on two pieces of data. As strange as it might seem at first, this is by no means excessive, since it is rarely possible to optimally encode module operations in order to take full advantage of these theoretical limits. For example, a given single-input, single-output module might require 3 control bits to determine a scale factor for the input, and another 3 bits to provide an output scale, leaving only 4 bits to select among 16 possible operations. Even though we still have 1024 possible combinations, not all of them are equally likely, and we cannot realize an optimal encoding in this way.

Low-level arithmetic operations make for very flexible modules, though the computational power of the synthesizer is hardly maximized in this way. Nevertheless, a simple set consisting of a 2-input ALU (arithmetic/logic unit) module, a 2-input multiplication module, and a 2-input memory (address and data) module provides an extremely flexible and simple set, capable of realizing virtually any synthesis algorithm, provided it does not require a large amount of computation. Even simple module I/O structures can be implemented with useful results.

Since the input to any given module may be linked via the control unit to a specified output of any module, module functions may be composed (in the mathematical sense) in order to obtain new ones. For example, if $m_{sq}(x) = x^2$, then selecting the output of this function as the input to another such function would allow us to obtain $m_{sq}(m_{sq}(x)) = x^4$.

Memory in an arithmetic module can be arranged for use as a stack, which allows the computation of results which require more than one operand, such as the product of two numbers. A stack is a LIFO (last-input/first-output) list; items are *pushed* onto the top of a stack as if it were a pile of pancakes, where only the top pancake is available at any particular time. Items can be *popped* from the top of the stack (removed), revealing the item lying "underneath." Typically, when the top two items on a stack are combined with a binary (two-operand) arithmetic operation, such as addition, the stack is popped and the top item on the stack is replaced with the sum of the previous two top items on the list. Modules can push values onto such a stack (the output, y, produced by this operation is usually not defined), whereas other functions can combine the input value with the top item on the stack in a number of ways. This flexibility provides a quite general calculating capability using a single-input module.

If T is the top element of stack memory S, we can define module functions such as:

$m_1(x)$	push x onto S
$m_+(x)$	push x onto S, add top 2 elements of S, replace T with new sum; then output T
$m_\times(x)$	push x onto S, multiply top 2 elements of S, pop S, replace T with new product; then output T
$m_s(x)$	look up sin(x)

We then calculate $A \sin(\theta)$ with the module operation sequence: $m_{\downarrow}(A)$, $m_\times(m_s(\theta))$, meaning first that we execute $m_{\downarrow}(x)$ with x set to A, then execute $m_s(x)$ with x set to θ, and finally execute $m_\times(x)$ with x set to the output of the previous operation. We might add one more function for computing a sum-of-previous inputs modulo some power of 2:

$$m_\oplus(x_n) = [x_n + y_{n-1}] \bmod 2^p$$

in which the output is the sum of the current input and the previous output (this function does *not* use the stack memory), and p is determined by the wordlength of the register used to perform the addition (the modulo operation is obtained by ignoring the overflow from the addition). Then we could perform the sequence:

$$m_{\downarrow}(A),\ m_{\downarrow}(m_\oplus(\omega_c)),\ m_{\downarrow}(I),\ m_\times(m_s(m_+(m_\times(m_s(m_\oplus(\omega_m))))))$$

This expression says first to push A onto stack S, then to perform $m_\oplus$ on operand ω_c and to push the result onto S, etc. The result of all these operations will be a frequency-modulated waveform with amplitude A, carrier frequency proportional to ω_c, modulating frequency proportional to ω_m and modulation index I as the reader may wish to verify. A repertory of just 5 module functions is required (namely, $\downarrow$, $+$, $\times$, $\oplus$, and sin), and 10 operations, of which 32 are available from any one module and 256 are available during each sample.

Under most circumstances, modules are more likely to consist of more specialized and efficient but hence rigid functions. As an example, the first implementation of the FRMbox actually included (1) an I/O module for receiving sampled data from the control computer and for outputting to the DACs, (2) a dual-input, dual-output oscillator module capable of either AM or FM modes of operations, and (3) plans for a rather complex arbitrary function generator module, again dual-input and -output, to provide amplitude envelope function generalization and other control functions. There is a clear tradeoff between generality and efficiency in such designs, and this is no surprise. An ideal mix of module functions would no doubt consist of a combination of medium-level functions such as oscillators, filters, reverberators, and so on, for efficiency, and one or more low-level modules to ensure sufficient generality to cover a large percentage of forseeable variations.

CONCLUSION

No computing structure is ideal for all applications, even those limited to digital music synthesis. Thus it seems that the closest-to-ideal structure is the most flexible, and the FRMbox represents a first step in that direction. Extensions to the FRMbox design are now being considered at the Computer Audio Research Laboratory at UCSD, the results of which will form the basis for a highly powerful and flexible machine (dubbed the DAP, for *Digital Audio Processor*) to be built as part of the real-time computing facility. The DAP will have a superset of the FRMbox capabilities, without being limited to a strict module visitation regime and fixed sampling rate. Further extensions are based on the desire to obtain as much efficiency while relinquishing as little generality as possible. Such machines which are capable at once of tremendous flexibility while computing very efficiently will, I feel, form the basis for digital music synthesizers in the 1980s, and perhaps for many other digital signal processing tasks as well.

REFERENCES

Alles, H. G. 1977. A portable digital sound synthesis system. *Computer Music Journal* 1(4):5–6. Reprinted in Curtis Roads and John Strawn, eds. 1985. *Foundations of computer music.* Cambridge: MIT Press.

Alles, H. G., and Giuseppe diGiugno. 1977. A one-card 64 channel digital synthesizer. *Computer Music Journal* 1(4):7–9. Reprinted in Curtis Roads and John Strawn, eds. 1985. *Foundations of computer music.* Cambridge: MIT Press.

Alonso, Sydney, Jon Appleton, and Cameron Jones. 1976. A special-purpose digital system for musical instruction, composition, and performance. *Computers and the Humanities* 10:209–15, 1976.

Mathews, Max V., and F. Richard Moore. 1970. GROOVE—a program to compose, store, and edit functions of time. *Communications of the Association for Computing Machinery* 13(12):715–21.

Moore, F. Richard. 1977a. Real time interactive computer music synthesis. Ph.D. dissertation, Department of Electrical Engineering, Stanford University.

Moore, F. Richard. 1977b. Table lookup noise for sinusoidal digital oscillators. *Computer Music Journal* 1(2):26–29. Revised and updated version in Curtis Roads and John Strawn, eds. 1985. *Foundations of computer music.* Cambridge: MIT Press.

Moorer, James A. 1977. Signal processing aspects of computer music—A survey. *Proceedings of the IEEE* 65(8):1108–37. Revised and updated version in John Strawn, ed. 1985. *Digital audio signal processing: An anthology.* Los Altos, Calif.: Kaufmann.

Samson, Peter R. 1980. A general-purpose digital synthesizer. *Journal of the Audio Engineering Society* 28(3):106–13.

Samson, Peter R. 1985. Architectural issues in the design of the Systems Concepts digital synthesizer. In John Strawn, ed. 1985. *Digital audio engineering: An anthology.* Los Altos, Calif.: Kaufmann.

5

THE LUCASFILM DIGITAL AUDIO FACILITY

James A. Moorer

With the advent of the compact disk and the proliferation of digital audio tape recorders, it would appear that digital audio will soon be available on a very broad scale. It seems only reasonable, then, to expect that the next step will be to digitize the production of the sound that these media carry. Simulation of the music production equipment currently in use requires a great deal of signal processing power that is not readily available on commercial computers at this time, but is now available on an experimental basis at reasonably competitive cost in a few places around the world through the use of special-purpose digital audio signal processors. In this chapter, we will discuss in general terms the problem of digital audio processing, and we will include some details on the device which we are developing. Along the way, we will summarize our design philosophy, which other designers may find useful.

AUDIO PROCESSING IN MOTION PICTURES

The sound in motion pictures is usually divided into three categories: dialogue, music, and sound effects. Sound effects are sometimes further divided into two categories: Foley and special effects. Foley (after Jack Foley, who worked at Universal Studios during the 1930s) comprises human nonvocal noises, such as footsteps; special effects include pistol shots, explosions, and everything else.

Although dialogue is generally recorded at the set, it is most often not of suitable quality and must be recreated in the studio. This entails an actor watching a print of the film and speaking the lines in synchrony with the film. The actor, however, usually hears little or no other sound cues, such as other voices, music, or sound effects, while trying to speak the lines. Needless to say, it requires actors of substantial talent to give convincing performances under these conditions. Some actors are unable to operate in this mode, so that recordings from the set must be used, regardless of their quality. Consider now the problem of the dialogue editor, who is presented with a stack of recordings, some from a studio (an acoustically dead environment), some from a stage (which can be very reverberant), some garbled or poorly recorded (with the actor facing away from the microphone, for instance). All these recordings must sound as though they come from the same environment—the environment that the viewer is seeing on the screen—whether or not that is what the recordings from the set sound like. This is all usually accomplished by ad hoc combinations of signal processing devices, such as filters, reverberators, modulators, and other tools of the analog audio studio. This is where the art of the dialogue editor lies.

Sound effect production is a complete art in itself. Often signal processing is added, with probably the most common forms being pitch shifting and phasing (feedback delay lines). Each sound must then be synchronized with the picture, which is typically done by splicing bits of sound between sections of silence. As if this were not enough, the sound editors are generally doing this work while the film editors are still making changes to the movie. Needless to say, when a film editor decides to, for instance, delete three frames from a scene, the poor sound editor must go through every reel of sound for that scene and cut out three frames. This is not so bad in most cases, but if a scene that has a background noise (like a factory or a train) is lengthened, generally it means that sound must be reedited (copied and spliced anew) to fit properly.

The final mix is often the first time when anyone hears the music, the dialogue, and the sound effects together. This is usually just a few months before the release of the film, and much too late to change anything substantially. The final mix usually has several tracks of dialogue, several tracks of music, and several tracks of sound effects. The mixing boards for commercial film work are quite large—a 72-track mixing console is not unusual. A console of this size is operated by a team of from two to six people. The most common arrangement is for the "head" mixer to handle the dialogue, and two other mixers to handle the music and sound effects. Typically, the mixing consoles have no automation, so that level and filter settings must be "rehearsed" in much the same way that musicians rehearse their performances. It is a fine art to balance the various elements so that the important aspects are brought out at the right times without distracting from the action on the screen.

If we calculate the number of reels of sound for every reel of film by multiplying the number of premixed reels by the number of reels that went into the premix and then summing over all the reels, we can see that a complicated scene can entail as many as 130 separate reels, or tracks of audio. Premixing is essential, then, as a way to reduce this quantity to a manageable number, although at the cost of introducing additional noise from the copying process.

This is the way that movie sound has been made for virtually as long as there has been movie sound. What we wish to do at Lucasfilm is to put a computer in the middle of all of this, so that each manipulation is precisely recorded and memorized, and so that there can be complete (and semiautomatic) sharing of information among the different mixers, including the film editor. To this end, we have designed, built, and programmed an audio signal processing facility that we hope will be able to perform these tasks with great efficiency and clarity of sound.

We might mention briefly that at this time we can only affect the production of the sound for the film. We cannot now expect to have a strong influence over how the sound is presented in the theater, since this involves both severe financial and inertial considerations that are beyond the capabilities of the immediate work team. Obviously, to fully reap the benefits of digital processing, theater sound systems would have to be thoroughly overhauled also. We hope, however, that we can help reduce the tremendous amount of handwork in film production (for example, splicing and resplicing all those little pieces together) and consequently lower the cost of film production (at least in the sound department). It is anticipated that lower costs would aid the entry of talented but underfunded creativity into the field.

This, then, is the background for our project. Since most of us on the team at Lucasfilm come from the computer music synthesis world, we have also embedded a great deal of music processing and synthesis capability into the system, with the feeling that when sound editors, particularly those involved with sound effects and music production, learn the true potential of the system, they will be seduced into using more and more of this power.

DESIGN CONSIDERATIONS FOR AN AUDIO SIGNAL PROCESSOR

A digital audio signal processor is a special-purpose digital device that takes in some number of digital audio channels—either directly from analog-digital converters or from some digital storage medium—and produces some number of digital audio channels as output, which are forwarded to digital-analog converters or some digital storage medium or both. The processor does to the samples whatever a digital computer could do to them, but does it much more rapidly (or perhaps more cheaply) than the equivalent digital computer could do. In the limit, the device might just be a single multiplication for each channel (gain control), or might include multiplication, addition, and limited storage (filtering, reverberation). More complex and sophisticated applications might include speech recognition or synthesis (a la "Speak and Spell").

The difference between an audio signal processor and a computer might be summarized as follows:

1. The audio signal processor generally has a much higher rate of arithmetic calculation than a general-purpose computer.
2. The audio signal processor must be able to sustain continuous input and output of sampled data for long periods of time (say, a full 8-hour shift in a recording studio) without interruption. (Note that one channel of 16-bit audio is 96 000 bytes per second. Eight channels is thus 768 000 bytes per second, or 1.3 μs per byte.)
3. Roughly the same program is run on each sample. In a dedicated machine, such as a digital reverberation unit or a hypothetical digital equalizer, exactly the same program is run each and every sample, although the coefficients may vary from time to time. In more general devices, we can imagine the program changing at a relatively slow rate, such as would be required to "patch in" a new equalization section "on the fly," but certainly less often than the programs in a general-purpose computer.
4. Although the total input/output rate is very high by computer standards, the computation exhibits great "locality," that is, each processing algorithm such as filtering or reverberation has great internal data processing requirements, but the high-speed (i.e., sample rate) communication to other processing algorithms is through a limited number of nozzles. For instance, an equalizer with four sections may have only one input and one output for a total of 96 000 samples per second coming in and going out, although it represents 1 million multiply-adds per second internally.

One might think that all the operations of digital computers, such as rotate instructions or exclusive-OR operations, might not be necessary in an audio signal processor. This premise has turned out not to be the case, although no examples will be given here. What is true, however, is that the amount of program storage can be much smaller than in a general-purpose computer, and that it is reasonable to be able to change this program at a somewhat slower rate than is acceptable for a general-purpose computer.

In our minds, the physical requirements for a comprehensive audio processing facility are the following:

1. storage medium for audio samples
2. conversion devices
3. audio signal processor, possibly directly connected to items (1) and (2)
4. control computer, possibly with its own storage for programs
5. console computer for input of real-time manipulation and generation of parameters (coefficients). This could be the same computer as in item (4).

Most of the work in the past has been on items (1), (2), and (3), but not on systems embodying all of the above items.

Similarly, for a general-purpose processing station that can serve many different purposes in digital audio, we require the following constraints on the audio signal processor itself. We will mention these requirements with only the briefest elaboration here; many of these points will be discussed in greater detail later in this article.

1. All algorithms must be in writable storage.
2. The system must be easy to debug. This includes a single-stepping capability and readback of most internal registers.
3. "Asynchronous" operation should be possible. This includes
   a. Capability of operating out of real time for complex tasks.
   b. Independence of DAC clock from microinstruction clock.
   c. "Graceful" degradation as size of problem goes up. That is, the size of the problem should have no a priori limit.
4. There must be numerical flexibility, so that multiple-precision is possible, some decision-making capability exists in the signal processor itself, and "other" functions such as exclusive-OR (or logical and arithmetic shifts) can be accomplished.

   Numerical considerations abound in any discussion of audio signal processing. About all that one can say with any certainty is that there is a problem here. It is our philosophy in this domain that everything should be possible. The implication of this is that multiple-precision arithmetic is essential, and that data-driven interpolating table lookup is a must for doing such functions as division, square roots, arctangents, and other important but seldom-used functions. As for decision making, conditional transfers are not essential, but some kind of conditional execution and data-flow switching based on computed data is sufficient.

5. The system must be able to "gracefully" extend power up to a very high level. This requirement implies some amount of "modularity" in each of the components listed above (storage, signal processing, control, etc.) with the ability to synchronize modules into a coherent whole. There should be no a priori limit to the size of system that can be assembled and synchronized.

Floating-Point versus Integer Arithmetic

The question of whether to use floating-point or integer arithmetic is fundamental to the design of an audio processor. The features of floating-point implementation might be summarized as follows:

1. The dynamic range is greatly increased.
2. The programmer need not be concerned about scale factors.
3. The hardware cost is greatly increased.
4. Error occurs in addition as well as in multiplication (in the most common implementations).

As to item (3), most designers conclude that floating-point implementation increases the hardware cost by about a factor of 3, if the device is to run at the same speed as an equivalent integer machine. Let us not forget also that one does not just compare an integer and a floating-point machine: a floating-point machine must also contain an integer machine for doing address calculation. Conversion between floating-point and integer must be as fast or faster than the floating-point operations themselves, if table lookup and A/D-D/A converter I/O is to be convenient.

Two things are necessary for multiple precision: (a) it must be possible to trap and use the carry out of the adder; (b) the multiplication must have signed and unsigned options for each operand separately. Any other features (division, shift after multiply, normalization, etc.) can be implemented in hardware to make larger, faster machines; but with the features just mentioned one can simulate, at some penalty in time, most of the processing that we have ever wanted to do. Likewise, the absence of these features absolutely prohibits many of the important algorithms, such as high-quality linear-prediction speech analysis, which requires multiple precision multiplies, and divides.

Just because we use floating-point arithmetic does not mean that all our numerical problems are solved. There are any number of cases where the 24-bit mantissa of the single-precision IEEE format floating-point number is not sufficient for audio signal processing; higher precision must be used (Moorer 1983). Simply switching to floating-point arithmetic does not eliminate the need for occasional higher precision. Likewise, it does not eliminate the need for programmer concern about scale factors and dynamic range, although such problems occur much less frequently.

The features of integer implementation can be summarized as follows:

1. It is easier to "tailor" bit widths in the hardware so that (for instance) filtering can be done without internal truncation.
2. In programmable integer machines, the programmer must be concerned with scale factors in every computation.
3. The hardware costs are minimal at this time.
4. The device can be designed to produce no error in digital filter calculation, except possibly at the output.

For these reasons, it seems likely that most audio signal processors in the near future will use integer arithmetic exclusively. Certainly all those that are in use in commercial real-time production at this time are integer machines. It is possible that hardware costs will descend in the future to a range that will permit audio processors to be floating-point devices, but we will probably be stuck with two's-complement integer representation for quite a while to come.

Throughput Requirements

Since McNally (1981) has described the design and implementation of digital equalizers in great depth, we will discuss just a single example: a digital presence filter. This filter is capable of boosting or cutting a single frequency band while passing all other frequencies largely unchanged. When the boost is set to 0 dB, signals flow through the filter unchanged. Although there is no a priori limit on the amount of boost or cut, specific implementations often impose practical limits.

Figure 5.1 shows the flow diagram of such a filter. Although this figure completely describes how to do the filtering, there is still the question of where do we get the filter coefficients b_1, b_2, a_0, a_1, and a_2. This is discussed elsewhere (McNally 1981); the point is that the calculation of the filter coefficients is not trivial. Given the specifications in terms of the center frequency, the amount of

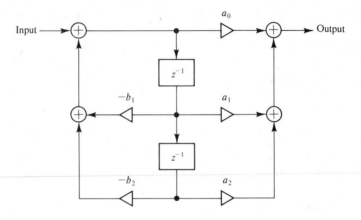

Fig. 5.1.   Flow diagram of the direct-form digital realization of a second-order section

boost or cut, and the bandwidth or Q, the coefficients may be uniquely determined by a relatively long calculation. Since these design specifications (center frequency, boost amount, etc.) generally come from manual controls manipulated by human beings, they can only change at a rate that is relatively slow compared to the sampling rate. It is generally considered that 1000 coefficient updates per second is sufficient for smooth, instantaneous response for even the most discerning of users, at least in the context of a mixing desk—music or speech synthesis may require somewhat higher rates. Thus we may think of dividing the filtering problem into two parts: (1) coefficient calculation, and (2) sample computation.

Let us say (without further justification) that calculating these coefficients from the center frequency, Q, and the amount of boost or cut takes about 100 multiplications. If we require this to be done 1000 times per second, we are asking for a machine that performs 100 000 multiplications per second. This number is on the outside limit of what can be done by microprocessors, and this is just one second-order section! One can imagine that for a more complex equalizer, the problem of coefficient calculation can become quite severe indeed.

Following this line of inquiry for the sample computation as well, let us consider the amount of computation that is required. There are five explicit multiplications and four additions. For the moment, we will not consider sample retrieval and storage, nor will we consider procedure call and return overhead. Let us concentrate exclusively on the arithmetic operations. Given 20.83 μs

(48 kHz sampling rate) for five multiplications and four additions, we can see that this value is already far faster than the computation rate of all microprocessors. Only mainframe computers have the processing power to do even one channel of equalization in real time. How, then, can we hope to equalize, say, 32 channels with four presence filters in each channel? This exceeds by a factor of several *hundred* the maximum computation rate of all but the largest mainframe computers, which are multi-million-dollar machines. To make things worse, this is just equalization. We have not included the so-called "outboard" equipment such as reverberation, compression, limiting, and so on.

Let us consider the throughput question from a different viewpoint. Suppose that this filter calculation represents roughly five multiply-add operations. To perform this 48 000 times per second requires 240 000 multiply-adds per second. Four presence filters, then, require 960 000 multiply-adds per second. If we round this up to 1 million multiply-adds per second, then we have a lower bound on the computational rate necessary for performing the tasks of a conventional mixing desk, which is about 1 million multiply-adds per second per channel. A modern 24- or 32-channel mixing desk, then, might require 24 or 32 million multiply-adds per second. Clearly, this will require special-purpose hardware.

OVERVIEW OF THE LUCASFILM STUDIO

Figure 5.2 shows the general plan of the Audio Signal Processor (ASP). An ASP contains up to eight Digital Signal Processors (DSPs). A single DSP is designed to handle eight channels of audio at a sampling rate of 50 kHz for professional music applications. Since movie sound does not normally have a full 20 kHz bandwidth, we may be able to reduce the sampling rate to 35 kHz, and thus increase the number of channels to 12 per DSP.

Inside each DSP, separate functional units deal with each of the main problems in this kind of device: (1) transferring data to and from the disks continuously at near the maximum rate; (2) performing the numerical calculations at the required rate; (3) transferring data to and from the A/D and D/A converters; (4) handling the synchronous changes to microcode and parameters. In addition, extensive diagnostic aids are distributed throughout the machine, allowing the machine to be single-stepped and allowing readback of most of the internal registers of the machine.

Each DSP is capable of a computation rate of about 18 million 24-bit integer multiply-adds per second. Since up to eight DSPs can be connected to a single DSP controller, a maximum of 64 channels for an ASP is achievable. The calculation of all these samples runs in parallel with a sustained disk transfer

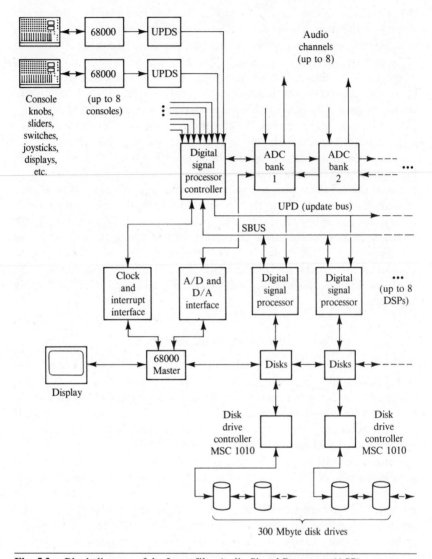

Fig. 5.2. Block diagram of the Lucasfilm Audio Signal Processor (ASP)

rate of 6.4 million bits per second (800 kbytes per second) and a sustained A/D-D/A converter transfer rate of 6.4 million bits per second.

The user interacts with the DSPs through one or more stand-alone consoles. Each console is connected to its own console computer (a Motorola 68000).

The Control Computer

The core of the system is a Motorola MC-68000 control computer, labeled "68000 Master" in figure 5.2, with 2 Mbytes of main memory. This is an improved version of the CPU board from SUN Systems. It supports memory management, including segmentation and paging. The board includes an interface to the 16 Mbyte (24-bit physical address) IEEE-796 bus, also known as the *Intel Multibus*. We needed a computer bus that many manufacturers supported (with memory and peripheral cards) as well as a bus with a relatively high speed of operation and a wide address space. A wire-wrapped disk interface card controls disk drives (up to 300 Mbytes each) from the Multibus. The computer system includes a mouse and one or more bit-mapped graphics displays with 800- by 1024-pixel resolution.

The function of the master computer is management of the audio processing stream through the audio processor. This task includes loading microcode into the ASP and linking it together, scheduling disk transfers and buffer allocation in the ASP main memory, handling exceptions (such as numerical overflow or hardware failure), starting and stopping the ASP, and global system timing. The master computer is generally responsible for what the system is doing at any given time.

The Master Controller

A high-speed controller acts as a sort of "switchboard" for up to eight control computers and up to eight DSPs. The controller multiplexes commands from the various consoles (through their control computers) and forwards them to the chain of DSPs (see section labeled "The DSP" below for further details). The idea of allowing multiple control computers is to allow for graceful extension of control up to a very high level. We have discussed already that the calculation of filter coefficients, for instance, takes a relatively small amount of time, but it still must be performed. To a large extent, we have delegated this task to these control computers. The controller also receives commands from the DSPs for A/D or D/A transactions and polls the appropriate A/D-D/A FIFO (first-in, first-out) memory.

Storage Requirements

We cannot afford to keep all the sound for an entire movie on-line all the time. Writable optical disks and other technologies offer an increase in density of several orders of magnitude over what is currently on the market; but until they are readily available, we must accept the solution of mounting and dismounting large numbers of disk packs. We thus currently plan to store the sound itself on standard 300 Mbyte disks. These disks offer several advantages, such as the fact that they are mature products that are easily available and easily maintained. If we consider a 50 kHz sampling rate, an entire 300 Mbyte disk pack when formatted in a standard way (32 sectors per track at 512 bytes per sector) holds 42 minutes of monaural sound. Since the 70 mm print of a film uses six magnetic tracks, a single pack holds between 6 and 7 minutes of six-track sound—in finished form. When you count all the material that goes into producing these tracks, it comes out to be many, many disk packs. The fact that the packs may be mounted and dismounted thus gives us the flexibility we need.

Each DSP has a dedicated disk controller capable of handling up to four disks (see figure 5.2). The controller is directed by the control computer, which delivers information such as cylinder, sector, and direction of transfer. Since each DSP has its own controller, there is no interference from one to the other; all controllers may be operated simultaneously.

Sounds in movies vary in length from very short (a whip snapping) to very long (background noise or music). Unless deliberate countermeasures are taken during the mixdown process, these sounds will be scattered around the disks in unpredictable ways. This forces a great deal of head motion to recover them all. Since the disk rotates at 60 revolutions per second and each track contains 16 Kbytes, a mean transfer rate of about 980 000 bytes per second (around 80% efficiency) could theoretically be obtained. (After the transaction is established, the data flows at the full 1.2 Mbyte per second directly to or from the DSP main memory.) Since we only need 800 000 bytes per second to provide eight channels of audio at 50 kHz, this mean rate leaves us some amount of margin for head motion. This fact implies that the buffer space must be quite large to allow for large, contiguous transfers to proceed in an uninterrupted manner. This margin is not enough to allow head motion after every sector (Abbott 1984a, Abbott and Mont-Reynaud 1984), so we must transfer some number of sectors contiguously. In our case, we transfer audio to and from the disk in units of 62 contiguous sectors at a time, which provides a reasonable compromise between the desire for access to very small pieces of sound, and for a large number of simultaneous channels of audio. We have 3 Mbytes of main memory at this time on our in-house machines; DSP main memory may be as large as 6 Mbytes. In this manner each DSP can achieve full 8-track record/playback capability at 48 kHz sampling rates without fail.

Note the difference in concept between this kind of random-access storage and traditional tape-recorder format. In multitrack tape recorders, one track cannot be moved in time relative to others ("slip-sync") without application of external processing, usually with an inevitable degradation of quality. In a disk-based system, changing relative timing is very easy. Similarly, to place the same sound in several different places on a tape recorder requires several copies of the same sound. With a disk, the sound may be recorded once and played back as many times as desired in any timing relationship.

The sound effects library at Lucasfilm is currently stored in analog form on 1/4″ tape. There are several hundred reels of tape. Some effects are monaural and some are stereophonic. Some effects are direct field recordings (such as airplane sounds or automobile sounds) and some are studio creations (such as "laser blasts" or "nose crunches"). If we consider for a moment the amount of data represented by all these tapes, assuming for the moment 16-bit samples and a 50 kHz sampling rate, we arrive at the conclusion that it would take about 100 Gbytes of storage (100 000 Mbytes) to digitize the library. After each film, the library grows by about 10 Gbytes since new recorded or created sounds are added. We concluded that it is probably not practical to store the entire sound effects library digitally at this time, but the day does not appear too far off.

The DSP

Each DSP is a horizontally microcoded 24-bit integer processor. By horizontally microcoded we mean that there are enough bits in the microinstruction word so that all the functional units in the DSP may be operated at once. This architecture results in a very high degree of parallelism.

The microcode memory contains 4K 96-bit words. The device is a lock-step, synchronous machine with no branching. The instruction counter starts at 0, goes to a fixed limit, then returns to 0. We chose this design for several reasons, not the least of which is that branching is not generally necessary in this kind of sample-at-a-time "stream" processing as long as logical and decision-making capabilities are provided in some other way (see below). Another reason is that with a number of DSPs in the system, it is very convenient to have them all working on the same sample at the same time. It greatly simplifies the interprocessor communication if this is the case. For computing recurrence relations, such as those involved in digital filtering, the "program" is the same for each sample. (Note: We cannot readily make use of the fast Fourier transform (FFT) for realizing these digital filters since most of them have time-varying coefficients, and the rate of variation sometimes approaches the FFT frame rate. We are thus forced to use the time-domain recurrence relation.)

The heart of the numerical part of a DSP is the multiply-accumulate unit, the scratchpad memories, and the buses. Figure 5.3 shows a block diagram of the DSP itself. The microcode memory and control logic are not shown.

Buses. Two 24-bit buses, called the *ABUS* and the *BBUS,* supply data to each of the arithmetic units. Each microinstruction has two 4-bit fields that specify the source for each bus, and a number of bits specifying which

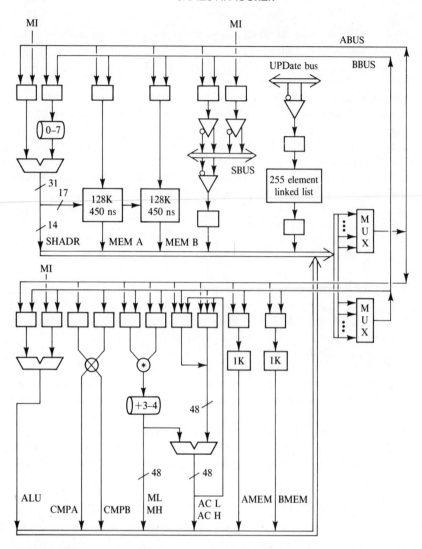

Fig. 5.3. Main functional units and the interconnection scheme in a Digital Signal Processor (DSP)

arithmetic unit input latches are to receive the contents of these buses. On each 50 ns instruction, two 24-bit data are selected from the functional units (scratchpad memory, multiplier, etc.) and forwarded, via the buses, to the input latches of one or more units. Any combination of functional units may be enabled to receive these data.

Two 16-input multiplexers feed the buses. (Some of the more arcane multiplexer inputs are not shown in fig 5.3.) For ease of programming, these multiplexers are identical. This design makes the buses largely interchangeable, even though some of the combinations will be seldom used. We did this because of experience with previous attempts to anticipate which paths would be used and which paths would not be used; in every case, further developments in signal processing techniques have proved us wrong. After gaining some experience with the machine, we will be able to look back over our programs and ask which combinations have not been used. With any luck, we can then reduce the width of the selectors in future versions of the machine.

The Multiply-Accumulate Unit. The multiply-accumulate unit, shown in more detail in figure 5.4, consists of a 24 × 24 signed/unsigned integer multiplier that develops a full 48-bit product. This is followed by a 48-bit combinational shifter that is capable of shifting left up to three places and right up to four places. The shifter output feeds into a 48-bit accumulator (adder and latch). This allows the partial products for a digital filter to be summed in double precision, permitting later truncation to single precision, or the use of even higher precision.

If the accumulate function is not needed, the direct multiplier output is available (to the bus multiplexers). The programmer may choose either the high-order or the low-order word, or may use the full 48-bit product. There are multiplexers on the accumulator inputs, so that three different functions may be selected: initialize to 0, accumulate (that is, use previous accumulator contents as input), and initialize to the contents of the ABUS and/or the BBUS. Furthermore, the output of the multiplier may be either added into or subtracted from the accumulator contents.

There are pipeline registers in the multiplier so that a full multiply may be started every instruction (50 ns). If a multiply-accumulate is started on instruction N (that is, if instruction N specifies latching either of the multiplier input latches), then the product may be selected onto one of the buses on instruction $N + 2$, and the output of the accumulator may be selected on instruction $N + 3$. For instance, to perform the filtering of figure 5.1 takes five instructions to start up and three instructions to finish (drain the pipe) for a total of eight instructions. These instructions are performed at the rate of 20 million per second (50 ns each). In a 20.83 μs cycle, allowing for other overhead, more than 400 instructions are available for processing, so more than 50 filters of the form shown in figure 5.1 may be realized. Note that since both signed and unsigned multiplication are available and the accumulation is done in double

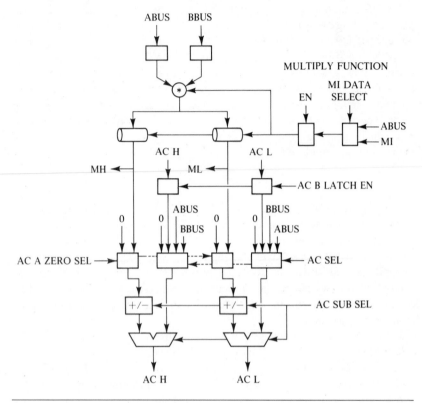

Fig. 5.4. The multiply-accumulate unit

precision, roundoff error is kept to a minimum and multiple-precision operations are possible (and, indeed, have been shown again and again to be absolutely essential). Since 24-bit precision is larger than the 16 bits needed by the converters, there is also enough head room to apply sophisticated limiting algorithms to prevent "wraparound" distortion.

Although the shift amount is normally specified by a microinstruction, it may also be latched from the ABUS. This option allows a limited form of data-dependent shifting, such as is needed for normalization or alignment of floating-point or block floating-point operations. Since the shift matrix has only a very limited range, large shifts must be synthesized in other ways, such as with multiplication by powers of 2. For doing normalization, one must first determine the position of the high-order bit. In this machine, this is most easily accomplished by the use of table lookups for large shift amounts, or through the compare/exchange units for lesser shift amounts.

The signed/unsigned feature of the multiplier allows simple extension to multiple-precision operations. It also simplifies table interpolation, which is used extensively in variable-length delay lines, such as those used in audio "phasers" or reverberators. Multiple precision does not have direct application in garden-variety audio processing, but rather in certain "exotic" possibilities such as modifying linear prediction of speech or deconvolution of room reverberation. In linear prediction, the filter itself can be easily realized in single precision, but the matrix inversion necessary for computing filter coefficients must be done in multiple precision for higher filter orders (such as those of order 45 or higher).

Since the DSP does not have a divide unit as such, divisions must be accomplished by other means. There are various schemes for implementing division, but probably the most relevant is a reciprocal table for some number of the divisor bits followed by some number of iterations of Newton's method for the low-order bits. Since the reciprocal is a seldom-used operation, even in matrix processing, this is not expected to be a bottleneck, but merely an annoyance. We have found that for a 24-bit number, a 4096-word lookup table followed by one iteration of Newton's method gives us 23-bit accuracy for all but the smallest (i.e., less than 1/4096) numbers. In this range, the dynamic range of the reciprocal exceeds the word length of the machine. If numbers spanning this range are expected, then some more comprehensive method must be used.

Conditional Execution and the Compare/Exchange Unit. Even in a "stream" machine without program branches, decision-making is still necessary. There are two methods for doing this: one is the compare/exchange unit and the other is the conditional execution of a microinstruction.

Figure 5.5 shows the data flow in the compare/exchange unit. A microinstruction can specify a test, such as comparing the ALU output with 0 or the two compare/exchange inputs with each other. All eight logical combinations, including unconditional TRUE and FALSE, are possible. A compare mask may be loaded from the literal field of the microinstruction word. Based on the result of the logic OR of all the bits showing through the condition mask, the current instruction may be executed or not. Likewise, based on this condition, the two inputs to the compare/exchange unit may be swapped. This latter feature is handy for control functions, such as filter frequencies that are being changed in real time. In this manner, we can specify a control function in piecewise-linear form, such that each segment has an increment, a current value, and a final value. When the current value passes the final value, the compare/exchange unit can be employed to substitute the final value.

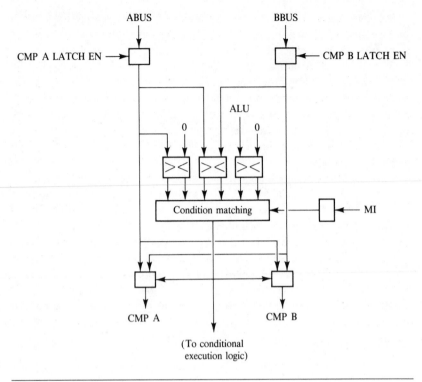

Fig. 5.5. The compare/exchange unit

Similarly, other piecewise-linear functions can be calculated, such as the absolute value of a number.

The conditional execution of an instruction is useful in several different ways: it can be used to reset loop variables such as the span, the increment, and the "twiddle" angle in an FFT calculation. It can be used to conditionally interrupt the host processor after a calculation is complete. In general, it is the "escape" mechanism from the lockstep nature of the computing engine.

The ALU. For doing all the other operations that are needed, such as Boolean functions, a general-purpose arithmetic-logic unit (ALU) is included. This provides AND, OR, and exclusive-OR, as well as addition and subtraction. Furthermore, a second register is included for accumulation of high-order bits in multiple-precision operations (that is, the carry bit is accessible), with optional sign extension of either or both operands.

Main Memory. The main bulk memory of the system is arranged in boards of two banks of 128K 24-bit words each. Each bank can be cycled simultaneously so that two 24-bit transfers may be accomplished in each 450 ns interval. Error detection and correction are pipelined with the memory cycle.

Up to eight boards may be connected to each DSP. In the normal mode of operation, we plan to use four memory boards for a total of 1M 24-bit words of storage. This gives enough room for adequate disk buffering with some space left for delay lines and table lookups. With the 450 ns cycle time, somewhat more than 120 memory references could be made in the 20 μs sampling interval if we started a memory cycle at every available opportunity.

There are two addressing schemes for the main memory. The DSP has an address calculation engine, consisting of a shift matrix and an adder to provide two-dimensional addressing capabilities. This is most useful for table lookup with tables of power-of-2 lengths. The shift matrix scales down the address so that the entire 24-bit range is reduced to correspond to the length of the table; then the origin of the table is added to produce the final address. The high-order 17 bits of this combined number are used as the memory address, and the low-order 14 bits (24 bits plus a possible 7-position shift) are available to the multiplexers for interpolation. This makes operations such as delay lines quite simple. Likewise, special functions, like square root or arctangent, can be accomplished to a limited precision by table lookup and interpolation. For interpolation, we might store the function values in one memory bank and the differences between adjacent values in the other bank, so that the difference and the low-order address bits may be forwarded directly to the multiplier for the interpolation calculation.

The second addressing scheme, direct memory access (DMA) from the disks, is asynchronous and is not under the control of the DSP microengine. There is a separate word count and memory address counter for this data path. The DMA operates on a "cycle stealing" basis, in that it uses cycles when the DSP is not referencing the memory.

The Update System. Processing a signal can be easily formulated in terms of digital techniques, since it mostly involves various kinds of filtering. Each sound, however, usually has its own "private" processing which is different from the processing of other sounds that might be going on at the time. One example of this would be two simultaneous pieces of dialogue, one of which was recorded in a studio and the other of which was recorded on the set. When the sounds are started, microcode must be loaded to perform the particular processing that is necessary for both sounds, and must likewise be unloaded when they are done (or slightly later if, for instance, the reverberation is to persist after the sound). For the duration of a sound, the microcode for that sound typically does not change, but various parameters (such as loudness or filter frequencies) will often change slowly with time. The implication of this is that we must be able to load a bunch of microcode at or near a particular time without disturbing any other processing (microcode) that is happening at the time. It is rare for all the microcode to change at once; more often, relatively small bits of it flow in and out of existence at various (precise) times.

Most digital audio processors at this time have the DAC clock tied directly to the microinstruction clock. This configuration is very convenient from a hardware point of view, but it makes it impossible to synchronize the converters to, for instance, house sync, as is necessary to lock a signal processor to a video tape machine (or movie projector). There are a number of gains in allowing the processor to stop occasionally without breaking the stream to the DAC. For one, the length of computation for a sample may vary. This allows one to, for instance, take a long time to set up a "patch," as is so common at the beginning of a new sound that requires its own special processing. Likewise, it simplifies doing things that are not exactly synchronized with any clock, such as memory refresh and disk transfer. Also, the DSPs run at many times the rate of the controlling computers, so it is not reasonable to stop the ASP entirely while the controlling computer makes changes to, for instance, the microcode.

To take care of these considerations, an update queue was included in each DSP; this is certainly the most unconventional part of the machine. Each entry in the queue is time-tagged and can be an update, which is a triple of memory name, memory address, and datum, or a WAIT_UNTIL instruction. The update queue is an expansion of an idea by Samson (1980, 1985).

The processing of the queue entries is as follows: at the end of a sample, each DSP goes into "update mode." In this mode, no processing is done. The head of the queue is examined. If it is an update, it is performed. These updates go at the instruction rate, which is 20 million per second. If the operation code specified WAIT_UNTIL, then the datum from the opcode is compared to the sample number. If the datum is greater than the sample number, then updates for that DSP will be halted, and the WAIT_UNTIL will not be removed from the queue. If the datum is less than or equal to the sample number, then the WAIT_UNTIL is removed from the queue and updates proceed as described above. Eventually, all DSPs either empty their update queues or come to a WAIT_UNTIL that is not yet satisfied. When all DSPs are in this state, the controller signals them to simultaneously start processing the next sample. They then fetch microinstruction 0 simultaneously and proceed through the cycle again. If there are no updates to do, all DSPs will spend a total of three instruction times (150 ns) in update mode. The total amount of time for each sample, if we include both processing and update time, varies from sample to sample. It is the FIFOs between the system and the converters that buffer the audio samples so that the converters may be fed a stream at exactly equal intervals.

The point of this complexity is that the 68000 microprocessor can forward changes that are to be made at a specific time to the DSP as fast as it can. When that time comes, the DSP will be held in update mode until all of those changes are made. The net result is that large amounts of changes can be made (up to 255 per DSP) that appear to happen entirely between two samples. This occurs quite often in the audio processing case, since typically some amount of processing (filtering, reverberation, etc.) must commence at the same time that a new sound begins. As often as not, this involves the "splicing" of new processing elements into the audio stream. As you might expect, there is a critical section problem here, in that if the splicing is done in the wrong order, quite audible discontinuities in the signal can result. We solve this problem by joining a group of updates into an indivisible unit so that all are effected at the same "time." Likewise, in order not to slow down the ASP, the changes are accumulated and effected at the natural rate of the ASP, rather than at the somewhat slower rate of the controlling computer.

As for the hardware required, there is an UPDate Send interface (UPDS in fig. 5.2) on each and every 68000 in the system. The CPU deposits four 16-bit words into registers on this interface. When the last of the 16-bit words has been deposited, they are forwarded to the ASP controller, and then to the appropriate DSP. There is no substantial hardware limit to the rate at which updates can be forwarded to the DSP. The only limit is how fast the 68000 processors can deliver them, which is a maximum of about 100 000 updates per second per 68000 processor. The DSP can handle a rate of more than 1 200 000 updates per second as a sustained maximum rate.

The ability to operate out of real time and the interface to a storage medium are part of the graceful degradation with mounting problem size. These are absolutely essential if we are not to box ourselves in to a device that can handle certain problems and not others. Our philosophy is that, as with programs on large general-purpose computers, larger problems may take more time but you never hit "hard" limits. Note that one implication for the hardware is that the microinstruction memory must be somewhat larger than is necessary for realtime operation, and another implication is that the machine must be capable of starting and stopping in response to I/O transfers.

This scheme has one problem, and that is with real-time manual intervention. What we have described above works quite well when the changes are known beforehand. If the changes are not known, such as when an operator is manipulating a potentiometer or some other input device, then the queue must be "short-circuited" so that the parameter changes may be introduced ahead of any timed updates that are already in the queue. It is for this reason that we allow updates to be entered at the beginning of the queue, thus going ahead of any WAIT_UNTIL that might delay its effect. Additionally, the queue may be edited so that new entries may be inserted at any position in the queue, not just at the beginning or the end. Although as many as eight computers can access the update queue, only one computer can be the "queue master" and insert WAIT_UNTIL instructions. All the others must insert untimed changes at the beginning of the queue. Otherwise, two computers that are not perfectly synchronized could insert WAIT_UNTILs that are not in order.

Data Transfer. The SBUS (see figure 5.2) is the "catchall" for data transfer. It is used to communicate among DSPs and it is used to send data to the DACs and read data from the ADCs. To communicate to other DSPs, one DSP merely writes a 24-bit word into its SBUS output port on instruction N. All other DSPs can then read this word on instruction $N + 2$. To communicate with a DAC, a DSP places the converter number (a 6-bit quantity) and an opcode into an SBUS function register, then provides a 24-bit datum to its SBUS output port. The SBUS controller (a global resource) automatically polls the FIFO for the specified DAC. If there is room in the FIFO, the 16 bits in the middle of the 24-bit word are placed in that FIFO and the ASP proceeds. If the FIFO for the specified DAC is full, indicating that the ASP is running ahead of the DAC, then the clock of the ASP will be suspended until the FIFO is no longer full. The situation with the ADCs is analogous. If the specified ADC FIFO is empty, the ASP clock will be suspended. These FIFOs are 64 samples long, giving a maximum delay of 1.28 ms to the audio path. In other words, this is the maximum delay between when a button is pressed and when the sound is actually changed.

There is another feature that we call the *bulletin board*. This is a 256-element memory that may be written by an SBUS operation and may be read by any computer with an update bus interface (UPDS in fig. 5.2). This provides a channel for certain kinds of feedback, such as the rms level of an audio signal or some overload condition. The controlling computers may also read back the current value of the sample counter and thus keep track of time.

Symmetry in Hardware Design. Several principles have been applied to make the machine as easy to program as is reasonable, given the fact that the machine must run very fast in any case. One of these we might term *symmetry*. The symmetry principle might be stated as follows: Whenever some element occurs twice, both of them should be treated as similarly as possible. Thus, in our machine, the A scratchpad memory and the B scratchpad memory are essentially identical. The A bank of the main memory and the B bank are identical. The A bus and the B bus may receive data from exactly the same sources.

We feel this symmetry principle is very important for programming, and we have tried to apply it wherever possible. There is a penalty for this choice, however, in that many of the combinations will never be used. The point is that this symmetry makes it possible for the programmer to learn to program the machine by memorizing only a few data paths, rather than learning a number of idiosyncratic paths.

There are certain places where the principle has been compromised. For instance, most functional units can take their inputs from either the A bus or the B bus. The multiplier, however, takes its A input only from the A bus and its B input from the B bus. This was done simply to reduce the hardware complexity a bit. In the ALU, the A input may come from either the A or the B bus, but the B input may come from either the B bus or the literal field of the microinstruction word. These few asymmetries were accepted to eliminate certain bottlenecks in the machine (bus bandwidth, board space limitations, etc.); but, as we said before, they were generally avoided in the design.

Occasionally, these asymmetries in the hardware cause a problem. In general, it is good programming practice in this kind of machine to keep all functional units busy all of the time. To do this, often you have to pass data to two different functional units on the same instruction. This is not possible, however, if both of the functional units can only receive data from the same bus. This is the case for the compare unit and for the multiply unit. You cannot transfer data to MULA (the "A" multiplier input) and CMPA (the "B" compare input) at the same time, since both data would have to go over the ABUS. An example of this might be calculating an envelope and applying it at the same time, since you would want to compare the current value to the final value and also multiply some signal by the current value. There is no problem transmitting the current value to both the compare/exchange unit and the multiplier at the same time, since the same datum can be selected onto each bus, but there might be a problem transmitting the final value to the compare/exchange unit and the signal to be scaled by the current value to the multiply unit if you did not take care to assure that they could go on different buses. In the more than 10 000 microinstructions we have programmed to date, there have only been a few cases where an extra no-op instruction had to be added because of a bus conflict. Generally, some rearrangement of the code can solve the problem.

Debugging

The machine may be single-stepped; most of the internal registers may be read back. Note that single-stepping is not easy. The interaction of the refresh logic with the main memory and the bus protocol are examples of places where activity must continue even though the signal processor may be stopped. If several signal processors are connected together, then their single-stepping must be synchronized. This allows us to debug a program by stepping through it one instruction at a time, and watching exactly which numbers are flowing through the machine on each instruction. This has proved invaluable for both hardware and software debugging. Similarly, we may allow the machine to proceed for some large number of samples, then stop either at a specific time or when a specific condition has occurred so that the machine may be examined or stepped thereafter. Experience has shown how important such a facility is (Moorer 1981; Samson 1985). It is hard to imagine how large systems could be developed without features such as these.

STATUS OF THE FACILITY

The ECL (emitter-coupled logic) prototype became operational in April of 1982 and is functioning reliably at the full clock rate. All of the complex features, such as the DAC FIFO mechanism, the DMA path to the bulk memory system, and the 24 × 24 multiply followed by the 48-bit accumulate, function reliably with a substantial amount of timing margin.

This prototype is a relatively large device. Each DSP is about 2000 16-pin equivalents. In fact, it is 1689 chips, but some of these chips are rather large. These integrated circuits are ECL 10K with some ECL 100K (not counting the main memory array). The controller itself is about 900 chips. Each A/D-D/A bank of eight channels takes about 450 chips.

We are currently designing the production version of the machine using high-speed TTL logic and a large number of gate arrays that are ECL internally but have TTL I/O (Moorer 1984). We are using this combination because it results in a substantially lower system cost with little loss in speed. It is relatively expensive to make the custom gate arrays, but the resulting savings in space and chip costs far outweigh the gate array setup charges. The production DSP will have a chip count of about 700 16-pin equivalents (counting each gate array as taking the board space of about eight 16-pin chips).

Our first customer for the production ASP system is, of course, Lucasfilm. A new film sound facility for the company is under construction on a site north of San Francisco. The facility will have a number of ASP systems, including two large mixing systems, two medium-size premix systems, and 22 editing stations.

Each editing station will consist of one 8-channel ASP, two 825 Mbyte disks (which were not available when the prototype was built), two 68000 processors, one touch-sensitive graphics screen, and a control panel that includes some small number of sliders and buttons. The ASP for an editing station will have one DSP and a controller capable of generating only two channels of A/D output. (Although up to eight disk files may be retrieved simultaneously in real time, they must be mixed down to two channels before D/A conversion in the editing station, since the editing station will only have two speakers.) There will be an imaging device, probably a video disk player and television monitor, so that sounds may be selected from the library (which will be stored in some as yet unspecified manner) to the local disk, then synchronized with the picture. As each group of sounds is completed (selected and synchronized), the schedule of which sound appears at what time is sent to the premix machine.

A premix machine will have four DSPs, each with two 825 Mbyte disk drives for a total of eight disk drives. These units will communicate with all other ASP systems by means of an Ethernet (which we call the Aspnet) for control information and a special point-to-point interconnection for audio data. The console for these premix stations will consist of 2 graphics screens, 16 sliders, and 64 shaft encoders (endless-turn potentiometers) and a number of switches and buttons. There will be two console 68000 computers and one master 68000. At this premix stage the sounds previously selected and synchronized will be placed in space (left, center, right) and any special processing, such as filtering or reverberation, will be applied. When this is done, the sound is sent to the mixing machine.

The mixing machine will have eight DSPs, each with two 825 Mbyte disks for a total of 16 disks. It will have 4 screens, 32 sliders, and 128 shaft encoders. There will be four console 68000 computers and one master 68000. By the time the sound reaches this stage, all processing and spatialization will have been done. The goal of the mixing machine is to mix music, dialog, and special effects together so that the dialog is understandable when necessary and so that, in general, the most important sound is always audible. Sometimes this requires addition of a modest amount of processing or editing, but generally not.

The core software system, including the preliminary console software, was written by Curtis Abbott (1982, 1985) and is being continually advanced and improved by Curtis and by Bernard Mont-Reynaud (1984). The editing and mixing front-end software is being written by Peter Nye, Alan Marr (1984), and Mike Hawley. The microcode for the ASP itself was written by James A. Moorer.

The prototype ASP has been used in actual motion picture production, although in the somewhat limited role of special effects processor. For instance, for *Indiana Jones and the Temple of Doom,* it was necessary to produce many background sounds from short segments of recorded sounds. Normally, this would be done using a tape loop made by physically splicing the head and tail of the recorded segment together. The problem with this approach is that the abrupt splice often produces an audible click. Although there are ways to get around this, it was easier to write a "tape loop" program for the ASP that records a sound of limited duration (5 to 10 sec), then repeats it with an adjustable crossfade between the end of the sound and the beginning. We used crossfades of as much as 2 sec to smooth out the transition. Another example of the use of the machine for this film was in doing "flybys." This practice involves panning the sound from one side of the screen to the other, simultaneously raising the amplitude to a maximum when the sound is in the center, and lowering the pitch of the sound as it goes by to simulate the Doppler shift for moving sources. Doing this in a conventional manner requires several passes through the sound to set each aspect separately. With the ASP, this was a single program with the flyby time, the pitch drop amount, and the amount of amplitude change all adjustable with sliders in real time. These were just a few of the effects that were generated with the ASP for this film. They were relatively simple ASP programs that saved great amounts of hand labor.

CONCLUSION

The digital audio signal processor presents a number of interesting problems in its implementation and programming, including numerical problems, the extreme rate of computation and I/O required, and others. In spite of these problems, the advent of digital audio in the commercial world virtually demands that the challenge of processing and production of audio in exclusively digital format be met. We only hope that systems capable of performing all these functions will be made following the considerations and suggestions given above so that we may not be made to suffer the reinvention of the wheel too many more times.

ACKNOWLEDGMENTS

The hardware was designed by James A. Moorer, with the exception of the main memory board which was designed by John M. Snell. The machine was built by the technical shop staff of Lucasfilm under the direction of Charlie Keagle (and a cast of thousands). The project was started in April of 1980 by George Lucas, and it is entirely his foresight and vision that have enabled us to proceed.

REFERENCES

Abbott, Curtis. 1982. Microprogramming a generalized signal processor architecture. In Larry Austin and Thomas Clark, eds. *Proceedings of the 1981 International Computer Music Conference.* Denton, Texas: North Texas State University, p. 264 (abstract only).

Abbott, Curtis. 1984a. Efficient editing of digital sound on disk. *Journal of the Audio Engineering Society* 32(6):394–402.

Abbott, Curtis. 1984b. Software for distributed real-time applications. Paper presented at the 1984 International Computer Music Conference, Paris.

Abbott, Curtis. 1985. Automated microprogramming for digital synthesizers: A tutorial. In Curtis Roads and John Strawn, eds. *Foundations of computer music.* Cambridge: MIT Press.

Abbott, Curtis, and Bernard Mont-Reynaud. 1984. Scheduling real-time sound I/O on ordinary disks. Paper presented at the 1984 International Computer Music Conference, Paris.

McNally, G. W. 1981. Digital audio: Recursive digital filtering for high quality audio signals. *BBC Research Department Report* 1981/10.

Marr, Alan. 1984. Lucasfilm computer film sound editor: EdiSon. Paper presented at the 1984 International Computer Music Conference, Paris.

Moorer, James A. 1981. Synthesizers I have known and loved. *Computer Music Journal* 5(1):4–12.

Moorer, James A. 1983. The audio signal processor: The next step in digital audio. In B. Blesser, B. Locanthi, and T. Stockham, eds. *Digital Audio.* New York: Audio Engineering Society, pp. 205–16.

Moorer, James A. 1984. A gate-array ASP implementation. Paper presented at the 1984 International Computer Music Conference, Paris.

Samson, Peter R. 1980. A general-purpose digital synthesizer. *Journal of the Audio Engineering Society* 28(3):106–13.

Samson, Peter R. 1985. Architectural issues in the design of the Systems Concepts digital synthesizer. In John Strawn, ed. *Digital audio engineering: An anthology.* Los Altos, Calif.: Kaufmann.

SUBJECT INDEX

NAME INDEX